The Aroostook War of 1839

The New Brunswick Military Heritage Series, Volume 20

The Aroostook War of 1839

W.E. (Gary) Campbell

GOOSE LANE EDITIONS and
THE NEW BRUNSWICK MILITARY HERITAGE PROJECT

Edited by Brent Wilson and Barry Norris.
Front cover illustration: *Fort Fairfield, July 1839* by Lieutenant Philip John Bainbrigge, Royal Engineers courtesy of Library and Archives Canada (G1139.71.P2B341840).
Firearms photos on cover courtesy of the National Firearms Museum and the Fredericton Region Museum.
Cover design by Julie Scriver.
Book design by Chris Tompkins.
Printed in Canada
10 9 8 7 6 5 4 3 2 1

Library and Archives Canada Cataloguing in Publication

Campbell, W. E. (William Edgar), 1947-
    The Aroostook War of 1839 / W. E. (Gary) Campbell.

(New Brunswick military heritage series; 20)
Includes bibliographical references and index.
Issued also in electronic format.
Co-published by: Gregg Centre for the Study of War and Society.
ISBN 978-0-86492-678-4

1. Aroostook War, 1839. 2. Maine — History, Military — 19th century.
3. New Brunswick — History, Military — 19th century. I. Gregg Centre for the
Study of War and Society II. Title. III. Series: New Brunswick military
heritage series; 20

E398.C34 2013   974.1'03   C2012-907751-8

Goose Lane Editions acknowledges the generous support of the Canada Council for the Arts, the government of Canada through the Canada Book Fund (CBF), and the government of New Brunswick through the Department of Tourism, Heritage and Culture.

Goose Lane Editions
Suite 330, 500 Beaverbrook Court
Fredericton, New Brunswick
CANADA E3B 5X4
www.gooselane.com

New Brunswick Military Heritage Project
The Brigadier Milton F. Gregg, VC,
Centre for the Study of War and Society
University of New Brunswick
PO Box 4400
Fredericton, New Brunswick
CANADA E3B 5A3
www.unb.ca/nbmhp

RECYCLED
Paper made from
recycled material
FSC® C103567

As I explore and research the past and learn how it shaped our present, I would like to dedicate this book to my contacts with the future, my granddaughter Calleigh Campbell and my grandsons Malcolm Campbell and Nicholas Jacula.

Contents

Prologue

On the cold winter's night of February 11/12, 1839, a diverse group of travellers gathered at the home of James Fitzherbert, in what would later become Fort Fairfield, Maine. In keeping with the custom of the time, Fitzherbert's home was open to travellers seeking meals and lodging. But this was no ordinary group of travellers, and what transpired that evening nearly precipitated a third Anglo-American war.

Among the travellers was Rufus McIntire, the newly appointed land agent for the state of Maine. He was moving with a posse down the Aroostook River, in what was called the Disputed Territory, driving away lumbermen who had been illegally cutting timber. Believing the "trespassers" had all fled across the Commissioners' Line into the province of New Brunswick, McIntire had left the rest of the Maine posse behind and, accompanied by three other Americans—Gustavus G. Cushman, Thomas Bartlett, and Captain J.H. Pilsbury—retired to Fitzherbert's for warmth and shelter. They were later joined by another American, Colonel Ebenezer Webster. Unbeknownst to them, the lumbermen had kept McIntire and his party under observation as they retreated across the Disputed Territory and back into New Brunswick. Seeing an opportunity to strike back, a group of between fifteen and eighteen lumbermen led by Asa Dow left their base at Tibbits's house in present-day Perth-Andover, New Brunswick, and made their way to Fitzherbert's. Arriving about midnight, they entered the house and captured the five Americans. When asked by what authority they were acting, one of the lumbermen, Punderson Beardsley, pointed to his gun and replied "that is my authority!"

The lumbermen placed the Americans in a sleigh and took them down the St. John River to Fredericton to stand trial. Meanwhile, Sheriff Hastings Strickland, the leader of the Maine posse, rode through the depths of winter to Augusta to deliver the news to Governor John Fairfield. Fairfield quickly responded by sending reinforcements into the Disputed Territory in support of the posse. When news of the capture of McIntire and his colleagues reached the lieutenant-governor of New Brunswick, Sir John Harvey, he warned the provincial militia for duty should it become necessary to oppose the incursion by Maine into the Disputed Territory. Fairfield, hearing that the New Brunswick militia had been alerted for duty along the undefined border, responded by mobilizing the Maine militia. The Aroostook War had begun.

Within days of the capture of Rufus McIntire, forces began to move that, if left unchecked, would have plunged Britain and the United States into their third war in barely fifty years. At issue was a boundary left unsettled from the American Revolution a half-century earlier, vast timber resources, and the strategic British line of communications that ran through the Disputed Territory to the isolated settlements of Upper and Lower Canada.

Chapter One

Origins of the Disputed Territory

[F]rom...that angle which is formed by a line drawn due north from the source of St. Croix River to the highlands... which divide those rivers
— Treaty of Paris, Article 2, signed September 3, 1783

The Aroostook War, variously referred to as the Lumbermen's War, the Pork and Beans War, or the Bloodless Aroostook War, is generally considered to have been a tempest in a teapot, and an almost comic opera-like affair. It was much more than this, however, and it was certainly more serious. Looking back over 174 years, it is difficult to understand why the Aroostook Valley, where a minor border crisis occurred in the depths of winter, could have become a flashpoint in relations between Britain and the United States. Yet it was, and though the subject of much mockery, the Aroostook War almost led to a third Anglo-American war.

The reasons for the confrontation were found in the Maine-New Brunswick border dispute, which began with the Treaty of Paris in 1783 that ended the American Revolutionary War and lasted until the British Parliament endorsed the Ashburton-Webster Treaty sixty years later. At issue for the new state of Maine was its inheritance from the Treaty of Paris, while New Brunswick wished to claim its share of what was considered disputed territory. But the key difference between the two sides was the British government's determination to secure the Grand Communications Route to the Canadas. In an era before railways and powerful steamships, the winter road along the St. John River and over the portage to the St.

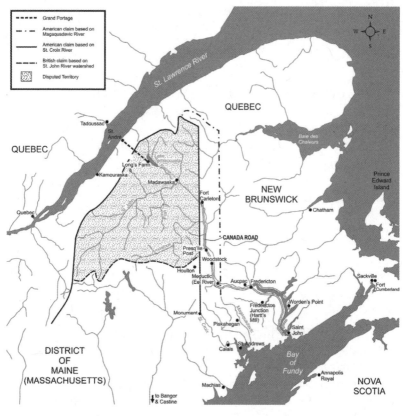

The Disputed Territory. MB

Lawrence River was a route of great strategic importance—and one worth fighting for.

At the heart of the dispute was about 12,027 square miles (3,114,993 hectares) of the watershed of the upper St. John River, an area now shared by the state of Maine and the provinces of Quebec and New Brunswick. Feeding the St. John in this region are several key tributaries. Moving upstream from the west, the more important ones are the River de Chute, the Aroostook, the Fish, and the Allagash rivers, all of which drain what is now northern Maine. To the east are the Tobique, Madawaska, and St. Francis rivers; the Tobique drains the north-central area of New Brunswick, the

Madawaska drains Lake Temiscouata and the smaller rivers feeding into it, while the St. Francis runs for the most part in Quebec. At the mouths of many of the rivers, including the River de Chute, the Aroostook, and the Madawaska, are falls; the largest in the whole system is on the St. John itself at Grand Falls. All of these falls present obstacles to transportation. Initially, the region was heavily timbered, with stands of tall white pine being particularly desirable. Cutting down the trees revealed valuable agricultural land along the river valleys' "interval" land that flooded most years, providing some of the best land for farming.

The area had always been a poorly defined frontier lying between colonial powers. Before the Europeans arrived, it had been the indisputable domain of the Maliseet people who inhabited the basin of the St. John River, known to them as the Wolostoq. During the French colonial period, the boundary between Acadia and the New England colony of Massachusetts was never clearly defined. It was thought to have been the Penobscot River—where an Acadian presence is recognized today by Acadia National Park—the St. Croix, or even the St. John, but no agreement was ever reached between the French and the British. For a while, after the British conquest of French North America in 1763, the issue of boundaries became less urgent. The boundary between Quebec and New York was surveyed and generally agreed to, but nothing was done to resolve the boundary in the remote area between Massachusetts and Nova Scotia, and since the entire region was now in the hands of the British, there was no urgency to settle the matter.

The American Revolution thrust the overland route up the St. John back into prominence, and it was left to the negotiators of the Treaty of Paris in 1783 to determine where the new boundary between the United States and British North America lay. They failed, mainly because the map they used—one that had been published by the Virginian cartographer John Mitchell in 1775 and updated in 1776—was largely based on supposition, not surveys; its details on Nova Scotia were especially sketchy. Moreover, the Americans sent their best team of negotiators—John Adams, Benjamin Franklin, John Jay, and Henry Laurens—to Paris, while the British representative, Richard Oswald, does not seem to have been in the same class.

Directed by London to reverse an earlier agreement to surrender Nova Scotia to the Americans, Oswald and his colleague, Benjamin Vaughan, had to find a boundary between Massachusetts and Nova Scotia that the Americans would accept. The Americans wanted that to be the St. John River, the British countered with the Penobscot, and the compromise was the St. Croix.

When finalized, the Treaty of Paris described the border as "from the northwest angle of Nova Scotia, *viz.*, that angle which is formed by a line drawn due north from the source of St. Croix River to the highlands; along the said highlands which divide those rivers that empty themselves into the river St. Lawrence, from those which fall into the Atlantic Ocean, to the northwesternmost head of Connecticut River; thence down along the middle of that river to the forty-fifth degree of north latitude." That description, however, immediately created two problems, one geographical, the other military. Unfortunately, the name "St. Croix River" was not then in use. The French expedition led by Pierre Du Gua, Sieur de Monts, had spent the winter of 1604 on an island in this river; Samuel de Champlain was part of this expedition and had mapped much of the coastline. By 1783, however, it was not certain which of two rivers flowing into Passamaquoddy Bay was the French St. Croix. The Americans claimed it was the easternmost one, the Magaguadavic; not surprisingly, the British claimed it was the westernmost one, the Schoodic, which would ensure that the village of St. Andrews, recently settled by Loyalists from present-day Portland, Maine, remained within British North America.

The Jay Treaty, signed in 1794, resolved a number of points of friction between Britain and the United States, and its article 5 authorized the formation of a boundary commission to determine which river was the St. Croix and to locate its source. Ward Chipman, a New Brunswick Loyalist and one of the three boundary commissioners, actively campaigned for the Schoodic to be designated as the St. Croix. By 1798, his arguments, mainly based on the discovery of the 1604 French habitation on the site of present-day St. Croix Island, had carried the day. Following this, the source of the St. Croix was agreed on and a marker placed at a site appropriately named Monument. According to the 1783 Treaty of Paris, a line was now to be drawn from Monument to the highlands that divided the waters flowing into the St. Lawrence River from those flowing into the Atlantic Ocean. Further boundary talks followed, but no consensus emerged on just where those highlands lay, and the War of 1812 intervened before any agreement could be reached.

The Jay Treaty also helped partially to resolve the military problem created by the Treaty of Paris. The St. John River was part of an important strategic line of communications that linked settlements along the St. Lawrence River with the outside world. This route ran up the St. John to present-day Edmundston, then followed the Madawaska River to Lake Temiscouata and Cabano where it went over the Grand Portage to the St. Lawrence. It had been an important route for the aboriginal peoples and then the French, but between 1763 and the outbreak of the American Revolutionary War in 1775 it had declined in importance because the Hudson River was a more direct winter route to the St. Lawrence. The British military rediscovered the significance of the Grand Communications Route during the war, as it provided the only contact between London, Halifax, and Quebec City during the five or six months of each year when ice closed the St. Lawrence to navigation. Yet the British negotiators in Paris seemingly ignored it, as the terms of the Treaty of Paris did not give the British clear control of it. In fact, a pro-American interpretation of the description of the boundary placed most of the route in the United States. Had the Magaguadavic River been identified as the St. Croix, the north/south line of the boundary would have cut the route to the west of Fredericton. As it was, the line north of Monument crossed the St. John just west of Grand Falls and therefore cut the route well east of the mouth of the Madawaska River. In short, there would be no all-British overland route to the Canadas, making them inaccessible during the winter months except through routes controlled by the Americans.

One cannot help but wonder why, given the strategic significance of the Grand Communications Route, the British gave away uncontested control of it by the terms of the Treaty of Paris. The simplest and perhaps most logical explanation is that British negotiators were not aware of its importance or, given the inaccurate map they were using, that they did not realize what they were doing. The British military were well aware of the route's importance, however, and after 1783 were determined to retain control of it, with the full support of the British government.

As the American Revolution was ending, Frederick Haldimand, the governor of Quebec, and John Parr, the governor of Nova Scotia, of which the future colony of New Brunswick was still a part, discussed ways to improve the route. In summer 1783, Haldimand called out the militia from the Rivière-du-Loup area to work on the portage road that ran between the St. Lawrence River and Lake Temiscouata. By the end of the summer, it was reported that the road was passable by carriages. Parr, for his part, had the route surveyed in preparation for establishing a regular postal service over it.

There was still concern, however, that the route was vulnerable to interference by the Americans, and measures were taken to defend against this possibility, the most important of which was to settle British subjects along it. The arrival of American Loyalists helped. By 1783 the route was sparsely settled by Americans of dubious loyalty to the Crown. Indeed, during the 1760s, farms along the lower St. John, freed by the expulsion of their Acadian owners, had been occupied by New England "Planters" who, in 1776, had risen in rebellion and laid siege to Fort Cumberland. The rebellion had been quashed, but now there was a new influx of Americans from New York, the Carolinas, Maryland, and several other former British colonies. This time, however, arriving as part of the great Loyalist Diaspora, they were indisputably loyal to the Crown, and after 1783 seventeen Provincial (or Loyalist) military units were settled along the St. John between Maugerville and Woodstock: the Maryland Loyalists, the 2nd Battalion New Jersey Volunteers, the King's American Dragoons, the Guides, the Pioneers, the New York Volunteers, the Queen's Rangers, the King's American Regiment, the Pennsylvania Loyalists, the 1st and 2nd Battalions Delancey's Brigade, Arnold's American Legion, the Prince of Wales's American Regiment, the Loyal American Regiment, and the 1st and 2nd Battalions New Jersey Volunteers. For administrative reasons, and because it was believed that the peace with the newly created United States would not last, these regiments were settled using a cantonment system. By locating each regiment in a specific block of land, it would be easy to mobilize them if war broke out again. This arrangement helped to secure the overland route from its start at Saint John to Woodstock.

The settlement of these loyal Americans along the lower St. John made life uncomfortable for the last pockets of Acadians in the area — in the Kennebecasis Valley and along the St. John at Aucpac, just west of Fredericton. While some of them had been granted the land they were living on, others had not. For the squatters, there was a real danger that they would lose their land for a second time. Fortunately, several of the Acadians, such as Louis Mercure, had been employed as couriers along the Grand Communications Route during the war and were familiar with the good farmland that lay vacant between Grand Falls and the Madawaska River. Based on this knowledge, the Acadians petitioned Haldimand and Parr, both of whose colonies claimed the area, for permission to relocate there. The two governors approved; not only would the moving of the Acadians avoid friction with the Loyalists, but their presence would "facilitate the communication" between the two provinces. When New Brunswick became a separate province in 1784, its first governor, Thomas Carleton, also supported the plan. The Acadians from Aucpac began moving there in the late 1780s and were later followed by those from the Kennebecasis. These British settlements along the St. John River represented the only serious attempt in the eighteenth century to colonize the river's watershed; unfortunately, those between Grand Falls and the Madawaska were located in what would become the Disputed Territory.

American settlement was sparser. After 1783, settlement in Maine, then still a district of Massachusetts, was focused in the southern areas and along the coast, since overland communications remained poor. The easiest access to the watershed of the St. John remained the river itself, which was now indisputably under British control.

The French Revolution of 1789 raised the possibility of a European war and once again highlighted the strategic importance of the Grand Communications Route, prompting the British to increase its security even further. In 1790, a militia company of Acadians was formed in the Madawaska settlement. The next year, two military posts were established along the route: Fort Carleton at Grand Falls and another at the junction of the Presque Isle and St. John rivers, just below present-day Florenceville-Bristol, which was referred to simply as the Presque Isle military post. These two "Upper Posts" served a number of functions. As Governor Carleton wrote, "by the chain of posts thus established, the Communication with Canada is become perfectly easy and safe, countenance and security is given to our extensive and flourishing Settlement of Acadians above Grand Falls, and there is every reason to suppose that the country between the two posts will soon become of consequence." The Upper Posts therefore served to safeguard the Grand Communications Route, to maintain the link between Fredericton and the Madawaska settlement, and to encourage settlement along the Upper St. John River. Still, not everyone agreed these posts should have been built. James Glenie, a lumber merchant and out-spoken critic of Carleton's government, complained about the cost and expressed concern that, due to the uncertain location of the international border, the posts were "within the limits of the United States."

Governor Carleton and other senior British officials understood per-fectly well that the boundary remained uncertain, but this did not sway the British from their goal of maintaining control of the route. When war with Revolutionary France broke out in 1793, the two British regiments in New Brunswick were withdrawn for service elsewhere. They were replaced by the King's New Brunswick Regiment (K.N.B.R.), raised as a provincial corps for service only within the province. The regiment was used mainly to garrison posts in New Brunswick, including those along the Grand Communications Route, where it provided security for the route and assisted the postal couriers who travelled along it. In 1794, the Boundary Commission established by the Jay-Grenville Treaty located the source of the St. Croix River at Monument, confirming the Upper Posts as being in British territory, thus securing for the British most of the upper reaches of the route and avoiding any immediate crisis over British occupation of territory claimed by the United States.

The 1802 Treaty of Amiens ended the conflict with Napoleonic France, at least temporarily, and the K.N.B.R. was quickly disbanded. Many of its soldiers received grants of land along the St. John between the northern

Presqu'isle, St. John's River, July 1807 by George Heriot. One of two Upper Posts built in 1793 to protect the Grand Communications Route, it was abandoned in the mid-1820s after the military settlement was established.

LAC C-012724

edge of the Loyalist grants at Woodstock and the Presque Isle military post, making the British vision of a chain of settlements safeguarding the route another step closer to reality. Meanwhile, Americans were beginning to move into the northeastern part of the District of Maine as the "timber frontier" continued to advance. In 1807, the settlement of Houlton was founded. Access to it, however, was primarily from the St. John River at Woodstock, a distance of about fifteen miles, and it was only when the Commissioners' Line was marked ten years later that Houlton was recognized as clearly within American territory.

While both British and American settlement was expanding in the area, little corresponding progress was being made on the diplomatic front. In 1803, a draft treaty, the King-Hawkesbury agreement, was drawn up,

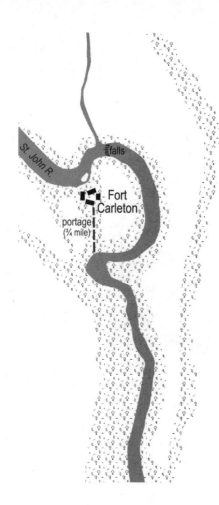

Sketch of Fort Carleton by Major Joseph Treat, 1820. The fort was built in 1793 to help secure the Grand Communications Route.

and in 1806 and 1807 further discussions took place, but they all came to nought. The resumption of war with Napoleon in 1803 soon created friction between the United States and Britain. Relations continued to deteriorate, culminating in a declaration of war by the United States on June 18, 1812.

The War of 1812 touched New Brunswick in unpredictable ways. In expectation of an early American invasion, the province's defences were quickly built up as new batteries and blockhouses appeared. American privateers attacked New Brunswick's coastal shipping and trade in the Bay of Fundy, but there was no invasion. Instead, merchants in the District of Maine negotiated an informal neutrality agreement that allowed them to continue trading with New Brunswick and to provide the Royal Navy and British army with urgently needed supplies. The Grand Communications Route continued to be used during the war by couriers carrying mail and despatches and, more important, to move critical reinforcements to the Canadas during the winter months when the St. Lawrence River was closed to shipping. The quiet nature of the land war in New Brunswick allowed the British to send troops from there to reinforce the more threatened theatres in the Canadas. In the most famous of these troop movements, in the winter of 1813 the 104th (New Brunswick) Regiment of Foot marched from Fredericton to Kingston, in Upper Canada (Ontario). The following year, a Royal Navy party consisting of 217 sailors and marines travelled upriver to Kingston to help man warships being built as part of the naval war on the Great Lakes. The 2nd Battalion of the 8th (King's) Regiment of Foot followed behind them.

This activity confirmed the importance of the Grand Communications Route in the British plans to defend the Canadas, but there was still concern about its security. Lieutenant Henry Kent, RN, noted that, while the sailors were crossing Lake Temiscouata they were "apprehensive of being cut off by the enemy, being in the territory of the United States." American agents did, in fact, make two ineffective attempts to interfere with the mail, and there was a report of an American spy being chased in the Woodstock area, but the route was never credibly threatened.

After Napoleon's defeat and exile to Elba in April 1814, the British turned their attention to the still-ongoing war with the United States. During 1812 and 1813, they had fought a predominately defensive war in North America; now, with victory in Europe, sufficient troops were available to enable them to go on the offensive. Part of the campaign plan for the summer of 1814 involved taking the war to the Americans by raids and major incursions along the coast. The most destructive of these saw the burning of Washington on August 24, 1814, and an assault on Baltimore.

Virtually absent from any account of this final phase of the War of 1812 is the British invasion of the northern part of the District of Maine east of the Penobscot River. Besides clearing out privateer dens in places such as Machias, this operation was also undertaken to "secure an uninterrupted intercourse between Halifax and Quebec." The Penobscot River had been one of the traditional borders between Acadia and the American colonies, and Sir John Coape Sherbrooke, the commander of the British forces in the area, intended to reestablish it there.

The first step was to capture Moose Island and the town of Eastport, across Passamaquoddy Bay from St. Andrews. A small, amphibious fleet under the command of Captain Sir Thomas Hardy (Nelson's flag captain at Trafalgar) arrived off Fort Sullivan on Moose Island early in the afternoon of July 11, 1814. Faced with overwhelming force, the American commander quickly surrendered. The next step was to secure the Penobscot River. On September 1, a British amphibious force reached Castine, at the mouth of the river. The outnumbered American garrison offered a token show of resistance, then retreated upriver. The British gave chase, fixing their eyes on the American frigate, the USS *Adams*, which had been damaged on a reef and was twenty-five miles upriver at Hampton making repairs. The British reached there on September 3 and fought a sharp action against the *Adams*'s crew and the local militia. The defeated Americans burned the *Adams* and fled. The British continued upriver and captured Bangor. Machias fell a few days later.

The American residents were required to swear an oath of allegiance to King George III or leave the area. Most of them chose to take the oath and stay, providing further evidence of the unpopularity of the war in the New England states. From Governor Sherbrooke's point of view, the invasion and occupation of northern Maine resolved the boundary dispute once and for all. On September 21, he declared that the western boundary of New Brunswick was now the Penobscot River.

Meanwhile, peace talks had begun in the Dutch city of Ghent. The need to secure the route was so obvious that, in March 1814, the legislature of New Brunswick petitioned the Prince Regent asking him to direct that the British negotiators ensure the boundary be changed to include the route wholly within British territory. Unfortunately, the Duke of Wellington thought that the inconclusive military outcome of the war did not justify any changes and, based on his recommendation, none were included in the Treaty of Ghent that was signed on December 24, 1814.

Wellington might have thought differently had the Plattsburg expedition not met with failure on September 11, 1814. As part of the British offensive strategy for the year, an army led by Sir George Prevost, the British commander in North America, pushed south from Montreal up the Richelieu River toward Lake Champlain. The Americans deployed to meet them at Plattsburg, New York. The plan was for the British fleet on Lake Champlain to defeat their American counterpart before Prevost attacked the American army's positions. The British fleet was defeated, however, and instead of shaking off this setback and attacking the American land defences, Prevost made an ignominious retreat. This setback effectively negated the other British successes that summer.

As a result, no territorial changes were allowed to stand. Article 5 of the Treaty of Ghent established a new border commission tasked with locating the border in the highlands between New Brunswick and Massachusetts. The commission did not start its work until summer 1817, however, and in the meantime the British continued to increase their footprint in the St. John River watershed. In summer 1814, Colonel Joseph Bouchette, the surveyor-general of Lower Canada, settled soldiers of the 10th Royal Veterans Regiment at the mid-point of the Grand Portage, between the St. Lawrence River and Lake Temiscouata, and at the mid-point between Edmundston and Dégelis (now in Quebec) on the Madawaska River. During the period from 1817 to 1819, soldiers from the disbanded New Brunswick Fencibles, the 104th (New Brunswick) Regiment of Foot, the 98th (Prince of Wales's Tipperary Regiment) Regiment of Foot, and the Royal West Indian Rangers received grants of land between the Presque Isle military post and Fort Carleton at Grand Falls. This military settlement, one of many created in British North America after the War of 1812, gave rise to the communities of Florenceville-Bristol, Bath, and Perth-Andover.

In 1817, the boundary commissioners, Colonel Thomas Barclay for Britain and Cornelius P. Van Ness for the United States, finally began their work. One of their first tasks was to survey the line — later known as the Commissioners' Line — that ran due north from Monument. By

July, survey crews had begun locating and clearing the course of the line. During the working seasons of 1817 and 1818, they appear to have cut the line as far north as the St. John River, just to the west of Grand Falls, which now forms the international border. Meanwhile, another Anglo-American survey party had been roaming farther north in their search for the elusive highlands. While this was happening, Barclay and Ward Chipman, a New Brunswick member of the commission, developed a new theory about the location of the highlands. Instead of being in the north along the height of land south of the St. Lawrence River, they claimed it was actually much farther south and ran along the watershed between the Aroostook and Penobscot rivers. This counterclaim, which would have granted the British all of the St. John River basin, including its tributaries the Aroostook and Fish rivers, led to the creation of the twelve-thousand-square-mile area known as the Disputed Territory. As later investigations would reveal, this area was rich in timber and much of it had the potential to be good agricultural land. Because of this counterclaim, the work of the boundary commission soon stalled.

While the boundary commission argued about the location of the highlands and the fate of the Disputed Territory, life went on within the area. The original Acadian inhabitants of the Madawaska settlement had received land grants on both sides of the St. John in the 1790s, but no more were issued after that. The settlement continued to expand, however, through natural increase and the influx of French-Canadian settlers from the St. Lawrence River area, although, under the law, those who settled on un-granted land were squatters. Massachusetts had also granted land in the southern part of the Disputed Territory — the Plymouth Grant of 1806, which would become Fort Fairfield on the Aroostook River — but no Americans arrived in the northern part until 1818, when Nathan Baker and several others took up residence along the St. John River, not far above the Madawaska settlement, and began clearing farms and cutting timber. Baker seems to have been the first to log on a commercial scale in the Disputed Territory. In summer 1819, he ran "4 large Raft of timber" down the St. John to market, illustrating that American commercial exploitation

Equipment used by New Brunswicker William Franklin Odell, the British surveyor on the Boundary Commission that cut the Commissioners' Line during the summers of 1818 to 1820. NBM 380186(3), 30145 (2), 301442

of the area depended on passage through New Brunswick—and New Brunswick brokers—for their products.

The early American settlers had a political as well as an economic agenda. Baker was quite vocal in his declaration that his group were living within the boundary of the United States and that American, not British, laws were now in force. This challenge to British authority was referred to Charles Bagot, the British ambassador in Washington. After discussion with John Quincy Adams, the American secretary of state, Bagot reported that Adams appeared "to think that the persons referred to…are, in reality, what are called squatters, and must be dealt with accordingly." Thus began the British contention that an understanding with the US government existed whereby Britain was to exercise jurisdiction within the Disputed Territory pending the resolution of the boundary question. Baker's efforts to establish American jurisdiction failed, and at least one American was charged with trespass, although the charge seems to have been dropped when he agreed to comply with British laws.

As 1820 approached, the boundary commission still had not agreed to extend the international border any farther north than the Mars Hill/Florenceville-Bristol area because of conflicting claims about the location of the highlands within the Disputed Territory. By then, the British had firmly established themselves along the Grand Communications Route and had a line of settlements, backed up by military posts and sedentary militia units, to secure it. With the exception of a few settlers along the St. John River above the Madawaska settlement, the nearest established American settlement was at Houlton, just below the southern boundary of the Disputed Territory.

On March 15, 1820, a new dynamic was added to the border controversy when Maine gained statehood. The transformation of the District of Maine into the state of Maine was a long and difficult process. The first moves toward independence from Massachusetts began in 1786, but votes for separation were regularly defeated. Maine's primary grievances were that Massachusetts had failed to properly defend the district during the War of 1812 and was neglecting it in other areas, such as education. But the agreement of the Massachusetts legislature was not the only obstacle.

American politics were sensitive to the balance between free (non-slave-holding) states and slave states, and granting statehood to Maine would upset this balance. The solution was found in the Missouri Compromise, in which Missouri was admitted to the Union as a slave state to offset Maine's entry as a free state.

An interesting feature of Maine's separation from Massachusetts was that the "wild and undivided," or public, lands of Maine were to be divided between the two states. This meant that the land in the Disputed Territory appeared on American maps as a series of alternating squares representing townships that belonged to either Maine or Massachusetts, much like the squares on a checkerboard. Having just won its hard struggle for independence, Maine was determined to have all of its inheritance, which included the fullest extent of the Disputed Territory. This became an unwavering policy of Maine no matter which political party was in charge. Each January, the governor of Maine included a comment about the "North East Boundary" in his annual statement to the state legislature. The tenor of this comment was a good gauge of how well the boundary negotiations were progressing. There were other factors at play as well. For the United States, this was a time of westward expansion. The eastern states were losing many of their young men and women to "Ohio fever," and although the phrase "Manifest Destiny" would not be used until 1845, and then in relation to the Oregon Territory, a form of proto-Manifest Destiny certainly existed and helped propel Americans into the new western lands. With the Maine-New Brunswick boundary not yet established, this same proto-Manifest Destiny called Maine's pioneers to go northeast into the Disputed Territory. In Maine the phrase "go northeast young man" might have been more apt than the one entreating them to go west. All of these elements combined to direct Maine's expansionist ambitions toward the Disputed Territory. Massachusetts, which had a half-share in the lands there, followed Maine's lead. These aims put them on a collision course with New Brunswick and, more important, Britain.

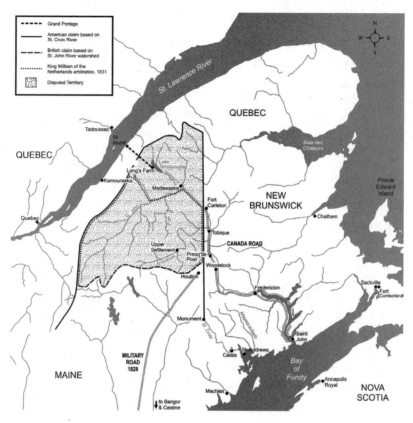

King William of the Netherlands's Arbitration Line, 1837. MB

Chapter Two

Maine Struggles to Gain Its Inheritance

To resolve our differences in a "spirit of forbearance and moderation"
— British Ambassador Charles R. Vaughan to
US Secretary of State Henry Clay, January 16, 1827

Cutting the Commissioners' Line north from Monument to the St. John River in 1817 and 1818 added a new dimension to the Maine/New Brunswick border dispute. Instead of an imaginary line on the ground, the boundary was now defined. But where did the straight line end and start to run to the west? Were the highlands far to the north of the St. John River along the heights overlooking the St. Lawrence or were they, as Ward Chipman argued, at the southern edge of the Aroostook River watershed? For the Americans, the line cut on the ground gave substance to their claim to all of the Disputed Territory, and over the next two decades Maine strived to make this a fact. British and New Brunswick politicians were content to let the dispute continue. They had what they needed — control of the Grand Communications Route and access to the vast timber reserves of the Disputed Territory. This implied responsibility for the stewardship of the Disputed Territory, a task they accepted in the absence of any effective American presence.

The first visits by American agents to the Disputed Territory appear to have gone unnoticed by the British. When the US government conducted its 1820 census, it included Acadians and British settlers of the Madawaska settlement because the settlement lay to the west of the newly surveyed Commissioners' Line, which the Americans assumed continued north to a height of land in what is now Quebec. In the same year, Maine sent Major Joseph Treat to "explore the public lands upon the St. John, and its branches west of the meridian line from the monument." His report provides an excellent summary of the state of settlement along the Upper St. John River.

In addition to exploring its "self-awarded" new lands in the Disputed Territory, Maine was also concerned about the illegal cutting of timber in the area. Maine and Massachusetts were keen to receive the revenue from selling timber-cutting permits, and the cutting of "trespass" timber did not generate any money for them. As in the past, all timber cut in the area was floated downstream and eventually sold in Saint John, so that New Brunswick reaped the tax profits. As early as 1821, however, Maine had land agents in the lower part of the Disputed Territory, including the Aroostook River, who collected fees for timber already cut and extracted promises from the lumbermen that they would not cut any more. The cutting, though, did not stop, and reports that increasing amounts of trespass timber were being cut, combined with rumours of expanded British settlements in the area, caused great concern to Maine and Massachusetts. Their worries were justified.

Not only was the Madawaska settlement increasing, but, since the early 1820s, settlers—most of them British from New Brunswick—had been moving into the valley of the Aroostook River, followed by British jurisdiction to maintain law and order. New Brunswick had also been issuing timber-cutting permits along the Upper St. John and Aroostook rivers, well into the Disputed Territory. This activity, which challenged their claims, alarmed Maine and Massachusetts, but the area's remoteness meant there was little they could do about it. In 1824, at Maine's insistence, the American government made a formal protest to the British about these developments. The British response was to state that they would continue to exercise jurisdiction there until such time as the course of the border was decided. In turn, Maine and Massachusetts responded in 1825 by sending their land agents, James Irish and George W. Coffin, respectively, to the Madawaska and Aroostook valleys to examine the situation. While in the Madawaska settlement, they offered to make land grants to settlers who acknowledged they were on American territory and to sell timber-cutting licences to the residents. Only two settlers, John Baker, who had inherited the property of his late brother Nathan, and James Bacon, both Americans, took advantage of the offer.

The visit by Irish and Coffin created an interesting conundrum. While the United States, at the insistence of Maine and Massachusetts, was urging Britain to direct New Brunswick to stop issuing timber-cutting permits in the Disputed Territory, the land agents of Maine and Massachusetts were busy selling permits in the same area. In 1826, the problem was resolved when New Brunswick, Maine, and Massachusetts agreed to stop issuing permits within the Disputed Territory. Meanwhile, the deputy surveyors of the New Brunswick Crown Lands Office and the land agents of Maine and Massachusetts would try to stop the cutting of trespass timber. The agreement, however, did not hold. By 1827, Irish reported that Massachusetts was once again selling timber-cutting permits on its lands, which left the adjoining Maine lands open to having their timber cut illegally or, in the language of the time, "to depredation." Illegally cut timber on Maine lands could be mixed in easily with legally cut Massachusetts timber, and the provincial and state agents were unable to prevent it.

The US government then lodged another formal complaint about Britain's lack of effective action to stop illegal timber cutting. In response, New Brunswick sent a magistrate, James A. MacLauchlan, to investigate. He concluded that most of the offenders were Americans who had received "indirect permission" from the land agents of Maine and Massachusetts to cut timber and establish sawmills. For its part, New Brunswick stepped up its efforts to curtail the cutting of trespass timber, in 1829 appointing MacLauchlan "Warden of the Disputed Territory."

MacLauchlan was to play a key role in the continuing boundary dispute. He warned people living in the area not to cut timber; if they did, their timber would be seized when it entered the acknowledged territory of New Brunswick. Since all the timber leaving the Disputed Territory was floated down the St. John River to the port of Saint John, this was the most important enforcement tool available. The seizing officers of the Crown Lands Office could intercept it along the Upper St. John at

James A. MacLauchlan, warden of the Disputed Territory from 1829 until after the negotiation of the Ashburton-Webster Treaty in 1842. Courtesy of King's Landing Historical Settlement

Grand Falls and at the mouths of the Aroostook, De Chute, and other rivers where they flowed into the St. John. But the ban was never entirely successful. Lumbermen ran the risk of having their timber seized, but when this happened they could simply pay a fine to redeem it. If they chose not to do so, the timber was sold at auction, but it was said that no lumberman would bid against another's timber at auction, so the original owner was often able to buy it back for less than the amount of the fine. Of course, the real goal was to run the timber past the seizing officers and thus avoid paying any fee to the government. In 1829, a Disputed Territory Fund was also established. Any revenues received from the sale of seized trespass timber were to be placed in escrow and the money divided on a proportional basis once the border issue was settled.

Meanwhile, two non-timber-related incidents occurred in the Disputed Territory that challenged Britain's claim that it had the agreement of the US government to exercise jurisdiction there pending resolution of the boundary question. The informal agreement had been renewed in 1826, according to British claims, when the British and American governments agreed not to do anything that would alter the status quo within the Disputed Territory as it was established when the Treaty of Ghent was signed. However, the American and British governments had their own interpretations of this understanding. For the British, it meant they continued to exercise jurisdiction within the Disputed Territory pending resolution of the boundary question. In 1825, John Baker received a land grant from Irish and Coffin, the Maine and Massachusetts land agents, which the British government did not recognize. In fact, the last British land grants within the Disputed Territory had been made in 1794, and the British had been scrupulous in not awarding any more. The granting of land by Irish and Coffin in the Madawaska area, combined with the insistence by Irish and Coffin that the Madawaska settlement was US territory, led Baker to declare, at an aptly timed Fourth of July celebration in 1827, that they were not subject to British rules. He went on to establish a quasi-republic and to then petition Maine for support. The British responded quickly to this challenge, arresting Baker and sending him to Fredericton, where in May 1828 he was convicted of sedition. There is no evidence that Maine was involved in Baker's "rebellion," but the state later reimbursed him for his loss of income; in turn, sometime later, the US government reimbursed Maine for its expense. Meanwhile, Baker continued actively to support Maine's claim to the area and remained a thorn in the side of the British authorities.

The second incident occurred along the Aroostook River, where settlers were accustomed to using either British justice or a group of their peers, known as "referees," to settle their differences. On September 17, 1827, Constable Stephen McNeil travelled from Tobique (present-day Perth-Andover) to the "Upper Settlement" (near present-day Presque Isle, Maine) to serve a writ against Joseph Arnold and to seize a cow in his possession. On his way back to Tobique with the cow, McNeil was overtaken by a group of thirteen armed men who took possession of the cow and threatened to arrest him. They also threatened the life of any British sheriff or constable who came back to the area. After the event, which became known as the

"Restook Riot," the thirteen men were served with subpoenas to appear in court in Fredericton, although it appears that the charges against them were quietly dropped.

The two incidents, both which were referred to as "riots," resulted in two separate American investigations with vastly differing reports. In one, S.B. Barrell, a special agent sent on behalf of the US president, determined, after visiting both the Aroostook Valley and the Madawaska settlement, that the British had been exercising jurisdiction in accordance with the Anglo-American understanding. Far from sympathizing with the dissidents, he urged the American settlers to be patient pending resolution of the border question and to exercise "forbearance and moderation." His report also shed light on the early settlement of the Aroostook Valley. Of the forty settlers living there, only nine were American citizens; the rest were British subjects who had come from New Brunswick, and many of them had fled across the Commissioners' Line into what they thought was US territory to escape debts incurred during a downturn in the timber trade. They were enjoying the benefits of living in a "no-man's-land" and the ability to select British or American jurisdiction, depending on which was more advantageous to them at the time.

The second report was submitted by Charles Steward Daveis, sent in 1827 by Maine to investigate the "riots." Not surprisingly, he justified the actions of the settlers and accused the British of harassing them, seizing their timber, and treating them as "trespassers and intruders on Crown Lands." The latter charge in fact was true, as, in accordance with the Anglo-American understanding, development was not allowed in the Disputed Territory. This meant that the Americans in the Madawaska settlement and the Anglo-Americans along the Aroostook should be treated as squatters and evicted; New Brunswick, in fact, had issued them with summons to appear in court in Fredericton, where they were charged with trespass, but the charges appear to have been dropped. The British in the Madawaska settlement were exempt from this charge, however, as their settlement had been created with government sanction prior to the 1814 Treaty of Ghent. The official reception the two American investigators received also reflected the state of the Anglo-American understanding.

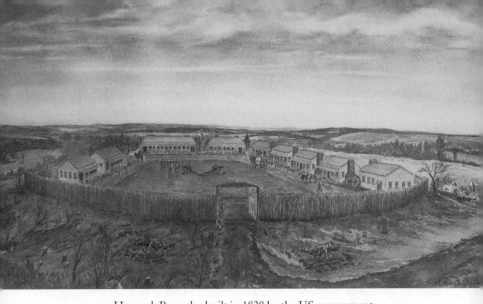

Hancock Barracks, built in 1828 by the US government
to maintain order on the fringes of the Disputed Territory.

With permission of the artist, Esther Orr Faulkner and the Aroostook Historical and Art Museum, Houlton, ME

The British — and by default the New Brunswick government — were not opposed to an American presence in the Disputed Territory as long as it was sanctioned by the US government, and New Brunswick recognized Barrell as an accredited agent of the US government, but not Daveis, who was only an agent of a state. In fact, Lieutenant Governor Sir Howard Douglas informed Governor Lincoln of Maine that he should address his concerns to the government in Washington.

The "riots" also brought on another, perhaps more significant, development. The nearest US town, Houlton, Maine, was just south of the Disputed Territory and essentially landlocked since no road connected it and the American settlements farther south. Instead, access to Houlton normally was gained through New Brunswick, along the St. John River to Woodstock and then overland to the American town. In the summer of 1828, Washington established a military post at Houlton, called Hancock Barracks, garrisoned by four companies of the 2nd United States Infantry, whose task was to guard US interests in the area and, critically, to build a military road linking Houlton to Bangor. The Houlton garrison paralleled the British occupation of the fringes of the Disputed Territory with their military posts at Presque Isle and Grand Falls, thus providing a counterbalancing US military presence in the area. It also gave the US government a post on the frontier from which it could monitor Maine's activities in the area while providing visible federal support for the state and for the US claim to the Disputed Territory. The road overcame Houlton's isolation and its dependence on communications through New Brunswick, but it was long and rough, suitable only for the movement of people and some goods; the key economic resource of the region — timber — still had to be floated downriver to market in Saint John.

These events offer a revealing snapshot of life in the Disputed Territory at the time. As the prohibition on timber cutting took effect, the commercial lumbermen and their sponsors in Fredericton and Saint John ceased operations in the territory. But efforts by New Brunswick to stop the cutting of trespass timber, to enforce British jurisdiction, and to prevent development of the area had led to resistance by the more recent settlers, resulting in two "riots." The government in Washington supported the British as best it could because the British were acting in accordance with its wishes. But the United States had to limit its outward appearance of acquiescence because it also had to support Maine for political reasons. Fortunately, this ambivalence was not to be put to the test for some time yet. Maine, on the other hand, opposed the British actions and actively took up the cause of the disaffected settlers. Then, as the excitement of 1827 began to fade away, a new crisis loomed.

By that time, the Boundary Commission established by the Treaty of Ghent had become stalemated, and the next step was to submit the case to arbitration. King William of the Netherlands was approached, but he was not the best choice. William had been installed on the Dutch throne in 1813 with aid of the British and was to no small extent beholden to them. Then, while he was reviewing the US and British submissions, a rebellion broke out in his country. British support saved William's throne and the House of Orange, although it also resulted in the formation of the new country of Belgium. In the arbitration, then, the British might have expected William to find completely in their favour. Instead, when he delivered his arbitration on January 10, 1831, he proposed a compromise that would divide the Disputed Territory along much of the line of the present international boundary. Of the approximately 12,027 square miles in dispute, 7,908 would be given to the United States (Maine and Massachusetts) and 4,119 to Britain (New Brunswick and Quebec). Although receiving less land, the British would retain control of the strategic Grand Communications Route, for them the minimum acceptable outcome. Judge William Pitt Preble, the minister of the United States at The Hague (and a native of Maine), immediately protested William's decision. Preble argued that such a compromise decision had not been in the king's mandate, and that he had been unduly influenced by the support he had received from the British during the recent rebellion. Preble returned to the United States, where he briefed Maine state officials before continuing on to Washington.

The Dutch king's decision meant that the British would get what they wanted — the strategic communications route — and the US president, Andrew Jackson, was also inclined to accept it. Jackson, however, was persuaded to send the proposal to the Senate for consideration, which gave Maine a chance to muster political support against it. Maine prevailed and, in 1832, the United States rejected King William's compromise. In doing so, Maine played the states' rights card by claiming that Washington had no right to relinquish land that belonged to Maine. The delicate point that, under international law, the Disputed Territory belonged as yet to neither country was conveniently overlooked. When rejecting the arbitration, the Senate did recommend that new boundary negotiations be resumed, but these proceeded slowly. There was still a wish, at least on the American side, to locate the "highlands," but realization grew on both sides that the two sides would have to compromise and divide the Disputed Territory between them, over the vigorous opposition of Maine and Massachusetts.

While King William's arbitration was being discussed in Washington, Maine took action to strengthen its claim to the Disputed Territory. On March 15, 1831, the Madawaska settlement was incorporated as a town within Penobscot County. On August 20, elections were held to elect town officials and on September 12 to elect a representative to the Maine state legislature. The American settlers and some of the French-Canadian

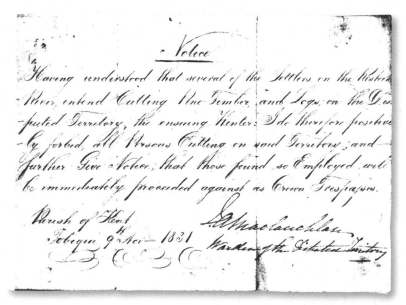

Notice posted in 1831, by James A. MacLauchlan, warden of the Disputed
Territory, to warn off trespassers; the land agents of Maine and Massachusetts
gave similar warnings, but illegal timber cutters ignored them.

Provincial Archives of New Brunswick RS 637 13f5

residents in the area appeared at each meeting. British officials Francis
Rice and Leonard Coombs were also present to inform them that these
elections were illegal, but they were ignored and the elections went ahead.
John Baker played an active role each time. Then, in summer 1831, Maine
sent John E. Deane and Edward Kavanagh to conduct a census of the
Madawaska settlement; they were also authorized to confirm existing
land grants and give new ones provided the residents declared themselves
to be citizens of Maine. Warden MacLauchlan challenged Deane's and
Kavanagh's mission but, perhaps to avoid a crisis while the arbitration was
being discussed, did not order them out of the area. Instead, he merely
accompanied them as they completed their census.

While MacLauchlan monitored events, the new lieutenant-governor of
New Brunswick, Major-General Sir Archibald Campbell, was not pleased
that Maine's challenges to British jurisdiction had gone unchecked. He

quickly set out to correct the situation, and in late September 1831 arrived at Madawaska. A British posse, led by Captain Leonard Coombs, was formed to arrest those who had participated in the election meetings. Four Americans were arrested and sent to Fredericton for trial, but the other Americans, including Baker, escaped. About thirty French-Canadian settlers were also arrested but released on bail. In the ensuing diplomatic crisis, Governor Samuel E. Smith of Maine said that, although the area had been incorporated within his state, there had never been any intent to hold elections, and he blamed everything on overenthusiastic residents. The US government accepted this explanation and requested that the British release the prisoners, which they did. Meanwhile, Maine reimbursed a number of the American settlers for their losses while in prison or on the run. Maine also reaffirmed its claim to all of the Disputed Territory, and warned the state militia to hold itself in readiness "to protect our territory from invasion and our citizens from capture," a statement that might be the source of the erroneous belief that Maine sent troops to the border during this crisis in 1831.

The next five or six years were relatively quiet in the Disputed Territory. Having mustered the political strength to persuade Washington to reject King William's arbitration decision, Maine was content to watch the slow progress of the new boundary negotiations and to continue supporting American settlement and activities in the area. The US government, meanwhile, held firm that any new boundary commission should be charged with finding the "highlands" and not to look for a compromise solution. The 1830s saw a downturn in timber markets, and combined with the efforts of Warden MacLauchlan and the land agents of Maine and Massachusetts, this greatly reduced the amount of trespass timber being cut. Even John Baker, the ardent supporter of Maine's claim to the Madawaska settlement, relaxed his stance and accepted a New Brunswick appointment as local commissioner of highways.

But irritants remained. Following the British example, Maine began pushing roads toward the southern boundary of the Disputed Territory, and surveyors from Maine and Massachusetts laid out townships and lots along the Aroostook River. Although they were aware of these activities, in the spirit of cooperation and conciliation, both the US and British governments overlooked them. This continued until May 1837, when Ebenezer S. Greely, whom Maine appointed to conduct a census of the Madawaska settlement, started his work. Washington then had surplus funds in the treasury and was going to return them to the states on a per capita basis. To receive its share, Maine needed to conduct a census of the state, which it asserted included the Madawaska settlement. Typically, though, Maine had not consulted with New Brunswick, and so Greely was promptly arrested for illegally conducting a census and "troubling the peace of His Majesty's subjects." Freed, Greely returned to his census and was again arrested. This time, the US government intervened on his behalf, and Greely was released once more. He then started his census for a third time, and for a third time he was arrested, stating that, if he could not conduct the census, Maine would send "another person to succeed him…with sufficient force to protect and support him in the act." This threat of force prompted Sir John Harvey, the new lieutenant-governor of New Brunswick, to write to Governor Robert P. Dunlap of Maine to protest the state's actions and to appeal to him to take action to prevent any "collision"—a polite term of the period for conflict—pending the outcome of the boundary discussions. Harvey added that he would have allowed the census had Dunlap requested permission to conduct it. Dunlap's response, however, was anything but conciliatory. Instead, the governor issued a Militia General Order declaring that Maine had been invaded and that the militia was to hold itself in readiness if called upon to defend the state. Harvey responded to this threat with a show of force, sending a company of the 43rd Regiment of Foot to Woodstock and another to Grand Falls in mid-September. This had the desired effect, and the crisis was defused.

In November and December 1837, a more serious crisis erupted. Rebellions broke out in both Upper and Lower Canada, heightening tension between the United States and Britain and its North American colonies. The rebellion by the *Patriotes* in Lower Canada was suppressed in late November after clashes with British troops in St-Denis, St-Charles, and St-Eustache, and many of the rebels fled to the bordering US states. The rebellion in Upper Canada was also put down in early December, and

1st Division of the 43rd [Regiment] crossing the River St. Johns, New Brunswick, on the ice, December 1837. LAC C-115855

again the rebels, led by William Lyon Mackenzie, fled to the United States, where they found many Americans eager to help the insurgents' cause. These sympathetic Americans, called "Patriotic Hunters," organized themselves into cells called "Hunters Lodges," and planned and carried out a number of raids into the Canadas and generally kept the border region in a state of turmoil. In early 1838, the United States Army raised the Eighth Infantry Regiment and stationed it at Sackets Harbor, New York to maintain American neutrality along the border.

The rebellions in the Canadas and the threat from the south demonstrated the importance to Britain of the Grand Communications Route and proved critical in establishing a *de facto* division of the Disputed Territory. As the St. Lawrence by then was closed to shipping for the winter, reinforcements urgently needed in the Canadas could only be sent overland through New Brunswick. The British were concerned that Hunters Lodges in Maine might interfere with the passage of troops, but no incidents occurred. The 43rd Regiment, which was stationed in New Brunswick, left by sleigh in mid-December and arrived in Quebec by January 1, 1838. It was followed by the 85th Regiment, the 34th Regiment, and the 8th Company of the 4th Battalion of the Royal Artillery. All of these men—so far the largest movement along the route—made their way up the St. John to the Madawaska settlement, and from there up the Madawaska River, across Lake Temiscouata, and overland to the St. Lawrence. None of this would have been possible had the American claim to the region been allowed: before the advent of railways and powerful steam navigation, there was no alternate all-British route to Canada. Without the Grand Communications Route through New Brunswick, the Canadas would have remained isolated and locked in winter's icy grip for six months of the year, and British authorities might have struggled to quell the rebellions.

The condition of the route, however, was deplorable. The Canada Line of the Great Road, as it was known, was open as far as Grand Falls, and there seems to have been a rough road between there and the confluence of the Madawaska and St. John rivers. To facilitate further troop movements, Lieutenant-Governor Harvey instructed MacLauchlan to have a rough road cut along the left bank of the Madawaska and to construct huts, or cabanos, at overnight stopping places where civilian buildings were not available, including sites at Dégelis and Cabano (both in present-day Quebec). Meanwhile, Lower Canada was working to improve the portage road from Cabano to the St. Lawrence. These developments greatly facilitated both military and commercial travel between New Brunswick and Lower Canada.

Harvey, also concerned about the possible American response to British troop movements through the Disputed Territory, arranged for the US government to be informed of these activities. The US secretary of state, John Forsyth, did not object, and forwarded the information to Governor Dunlap in the Maine state capital, Augusta. Maine also made no attempt to interfere, and Harvey responded by releasing would-be census taker Greely in February 1838. Nevertheless, a joint select committee of the

Maine legislature declared that the troop movements were "a palpable outrage on the sovereignty of Maine, and of the United States, and a fresh cause of complaint."

Border tensions flared anew in November 1838 when another rebellion broke out in Lower Canada and a party of American Patriotic Hunters attacked Prescott, on the St. Lawrence in Upper Canada, landing on November 12 to the east of the town and occupying a stone windmill. The British, both regulars and militia, quickly responded, defeating the Hunters in the Battle of the Windmill, which took place from November 12 to 16. Once more, reinforcements were urgently needed and again they travelled to the Canadas over the Grand Communications Route. The 11th Regiment, a company from each the 65th and 95th Regiments, and the 1st Company of the 4th Battalion of the Royal Artillery used the route between late December 1838 and early January 1839.

The Greely incident and the troop movements put relations between New Brunswick and Maine on edge, although both sides tried to avoid a collision. The United States and Britain again considered ways to settle the boundary issue, either by a new survey to locate the "highlands" or by a compromise solution. Maine, though, immediately rejected any possibility of a compromise and reasserted its claim to all of the Disputed Territory. In addition, an upturn in the timber market prompted the timber merchants of Saint John, Fredericton, and Woodstock to begin sending men into the Disputed Territory to cut timber. As well, it was becoming increasingly difficult to separate illegal timber from legal, particularly as, in a time of economic hardship, settlers were allowed to cut and sell small quantities of timber to support their families. Legally cut timber was also coming down the Madawaska and the St. John from the Lake Temiscouata region, which made it easier to smuggle out trespass timber disguised as legal timber. The problem was further complicated by the selling by Massachusetts of timber-cutting rights on the headwaters of the Aroostook River, much to Maine's displeasure. The land agents of Maine and Massachusetts, MacLauchlan, the warden of the Disputed Territory, and seizing officers from the Crown Lands Office all worked to curb the illegal cutting, but with limited success. They could not count on the support of the settlers, who seemed to be just as involved in cutting trespass timber as were the outside lumbermen. Good timber was to be had in the Disputed Territory, and the potential profits justified the risks.

As 1838 drew to a close, a series of cross-border irritants was raising tensions to the boiling point. In Maine, the Greely crisis and troop movements had generated strong anti-British feelings. The illegal cutting of timber, always a source of friction, was on the rise, and authorities on both sides of the Commissioners' Line seemed unable to stop it. The new Anglo-American boundary discussions were now considering the possibility of a compromise solution instead of that described in the Treaty of Paris. Although it had put an end to King William's compromise arbitration, Maine looked as though it might have to fight the battle a second time. It was also election time in the state, and the race for governor was between the incumbent Whig, Edward Kent, and his challenger, John Fairfield, a Democrat. The British and US governments were committed to a policy of cooperation and conciliation pending a peaceful resolution of the boundary issue, but events were starting to move beyond their control.

Chapter Three

The Maine Armed Posse Encounters the Lumbermen's Resistance

That is my authority
— Punderson Beardsley to Colonel Ebenezer Webster,
February 12, 1839, in reference to the firearm in his hand

No one expected 1839 to begin with an international crisis in the Disputed Territory, and yet it did. The traditional reasons given for this crisis, known as the Aroostook War, are political rivalries within Maine and concern about a report predicting an alarming increase in the cutting of trespass timber. While valid, and perhaps the most visible explanations for the crisis, they are not the only reasons Maine initiated action that threatened to plunge Britain and the United States into war. The salient features remained the still-unresolved border and the exercise of British jurisdiction pending the outcome of the dispute. That the majority of settlers in the area were British subjects further complicated matters. So, too, did Maine's precarious financial state: the legislature in Augusta could ill afford the loss of revenue brought about by the sale of trespass timber through New Brunswick.

Boundary negotiations between Britain and the United States effectively had stopped in 1832, when the latter rejected the arbitration decision of King William of the Netherlands. On receiving this news, Maine's governor, Edward Kent, had formed a joint select committee to review the state's position. The committee's report upheld Maine's claim to all of the Disputed Territory, which would have drawn the line east of the Madawaska settlement and effectively severed the only winter route between Britain's Maritime provinces and the Canadas. On March 23,

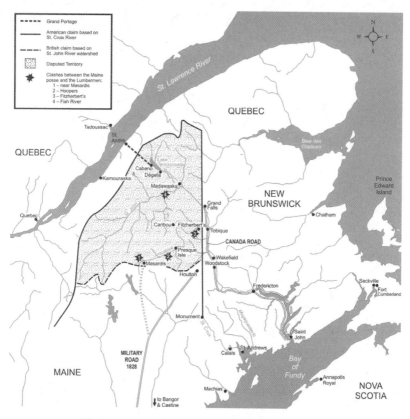

Legend:
- Grand Portage
- American claim based on St. Croix River
- British claim based on St. John River watershed
- Disputed Territory
- Clashes between the Maine posse and the Lumbermen:
  1 – near Masardis
  2 – Hoopers
  3 – Fitzherbert's
  4 – Fish River

Clashes between the Maine posse and lumbermen. 175

1838, Maine passed a Resolve which stated that it would "insist on the line established by the Treaty of 1783." Maine also sent out a party to survey the area north of the St. John River. Not surprisingly, the results of the survey party — led by John Deane and including James Irish, a former Maine land agent, and surveyor William P. Parrot — confirmed the claim of the United States, and subsequently that of Maine, to all of the Disputed Territory. While in the upper half of the Disputed Territory, Deane also investigated reports of illegal timber cutting in the country north of Grand Falls and around the Grand Communications Route, and found the practice to be widespread. Feeling that British enforcement was ineffective, he wrote that "our forests have been and are now being stripped" of the good, easily accessible timber, and wondered "how long will Maine submit and allow the pres[ent] system to go on." Deane also learned that Captain Hawkshaw of the Royal Engineers had been in the Madawaska settlement for the reported purpose of scouting sites for future fortifications, and was informed that in the coming months more troops would be passing along the route to Canada. Both the outgoing governor, Kent, and his successor, John Fairfield, were aware of Deane's report.

The issue of the Disputed Territory had important financial repercussions for Maine, which had hitched its financial strategy to the sale of public lands. In 1835, the state was in the midst of a land speculation bubble, with revenue from the sale of land totalling $335,478.32, of which $133,567 was deposited in the state treasury—a sharp increase from the $31,000 that had been deposited the previous year—while the rest remained as promissory notes. As a result of this windfall, instead of adding the revenue from its bank tax to the treasury, Maine diverted the money to support schools and stopped collecting the state tax on estates and polls altogether. Unfortunately, the land bubble burst the following year, with land sales realizing only $44,000 for the treasury, and in 1837 a general economic depression set in. Maine resisted reviving the state tax, however, with the state treasurer declaring that "[d]irect taxation is the most odious and most expensive way of sustaining the government. It should be avoided if possible." Instead, Maine began borrowing money to keep itself solvent, and the state debt grew from $55,000 in 1835, to $135,000 in 1836, $281,000 in 1837, and $584,000 in 1838. Moreover, the state found it could not borrow money except at usurious rates of 15 to 20 percent. By the end of 1839, the debt would grow to $1,187,000 and claims against the state would not be paid.

When he took office in early January 1839, Governor John Fairfield was well aware that Maine desperately needed money and that the best source was the rich timber and agricultural lands of the Disputed Territory. The state had recently renewed its claim to all of the area, but it was quite evident that the British were firmly entrenched in the northern half and were not going to give it up. This left only the southern section still in dispute, since neither side had a permanent presence there. The only practical access remained through New Brunswick using the St. John River or the road paralleling it. Maine and Massachusetts were building a road north from Bangor that would eventually emerge at Fish River on the St. John River, twenty miles upriver from where the Madawaska River entered. But progress was slow, and by 1839 the road (the future Maine Route 11) was only approaching the southern boundary of the Disputed Territory. It must have been plain to Maine politicians that a boundary settlement would soon be reached and that, if Maine did not take firm action to secure its claim, all or most of the Disputed Territory might be lost.

The dispute highlighted the political rivalry between Maine's Whigs and Democrats, which can be seen in Fairfield's address to the state legislature on January 4, 1839. No doubt frustrated by the lack of effective action by the previous Whig administration, Fairfield said "[w]e are not remediless. If Maine should take possession of her territory, up to the line of the treaty of 1783, resolved to maintain it with all the force she is capable of exerting, any attempt on the part of the British government to wrest that possession from her must bring the general government [of the United States] to her aid and defense.... This step, however, is only to be taken after mature deliberation. Once taken, it can never be abandoned!" These were strong words, and events would soon give Fairfield the chance to show if he was prepared to back them with action.

The New Brunswick government was aware of these developments in Maine and, through frequent dispatches sent from Fredericton to London, so was the British government. The newspapers of the day, moreover, were quite candid in their reporting of the events taking place in the state legislature in Augusta. Overall, the British were satisfied with the state of affairs in the Disputed Territory. They had effectively occupied the northern part, including both sides of the St. John River as it flowed through the Madawaska settlement, and their policy of planned military and civilian settlements had secured the Grand Communications Route. Despite the ban on timber cutting in the Disputed Territory, timber was floating downriver to the markets in Saint John. Although the area around Lake Temiscouata was technically within the Disputed Territory and subject to

Maine, Public Debt, 1832 - 1839

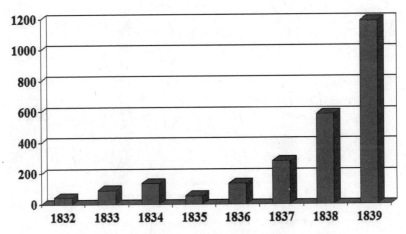

Maine's public debt rose rapidly during the 1830s, causing its
politicians to look toward the timber of the Disputed Territory
as a source of badly needed revenue.

the cutting ban, this was simply overlooked and timber from there added
to the flow down the St. John. Best of all, by introducing the counterclaim
that the "highlands" were along the southern edge of the watershed of the
Aroostook River, the British had created a buffer between the Americans
and the strategically important northern portion of the Disputed Territory.
There was reason to be confident that Washington eventually would realize
that a compromise border was the only viable solution and that the Grand
Communications Route would be secured by international treaty. As for
Fairfield's comments, the British were accustomed to strong rhetoric from
Maine politicians, especially when the border dispute was mentioned.

Although selling timber-cutting permits promised Maine a revenue
windfall, the economic downturn in the mid-1830s actually eased tension
in the Disputed Territory. As the timber market picked up, however, relations deteriorated once more. Nevertheless, in October 1838, Elijah L.

Estimated Quantity of Trespass Timber Cut, 1832 - 1839 (Tons)

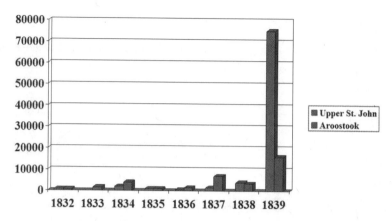

Buckmore's January 1839 forecast of trespass or illegal timber cutting was either an exaggeration or an attempt to create a *casus bellus*.

Hamlin, the Maine land agent, visited the Aroostook valley and warned off a number of crews that were beginning to cut. While there, he met MacLauchlan, who was performing the same duty for New Brunswick. The positive results of this visit led Hamlin to believe that cutting trespass timber would not be a problem during the coming winter. He and George W. Coffin, the Massachusetts land agent, authorized George W. Buckmore to monitor the situation over the winter and to prevent the cutting of trespass timber on the Aroostook and Fish rivers. This was not the first time that the land agents had left a watchman in the Aroostook Valley; Dennis Fairbanks, who had a farm and mill near present-day Presque Isle, had performed this task on several occasions. His successor, however, was to be more controversial.

In late December, Buckmore made an inspection tour of the area and presented a report that could only be described as sensational. The amount of reported trespass timber cut the year before was about 3,400 tons along the Aroostook and 4,000 tons along the Upper St. John. These were modest figures and the key reason Hamlin and MacLauchlan had agreed that there was no real crisis in the area. Buckmore's report shattered this complacency. He found that large-scale cutting was taking place along the St. John and its tributaries above Grand Falls, and estimated that at least 75,000 tons would be cut in the northern Disputed Territory, the area firmly under British jurisdiction, with about 25,000 tons of it coming from the Fish River. Buckmore then proceeded to the Aroostook River, where he found a similar situation. The main focus seemed to be along one tributary, the Little Madawaska, which joins the Aroostook near the present-day town of Caribou. Buckmore estimated that the several crews working there would cut between 15,000 and 20,000 tons of timber. Moreover, lumbermen working along the Aroostook told him they would not stop cutting and would resist any attempt to make them stop or remove their teams.

Back in Augusta, Buckmore submitted his report to Hamlin on January 22, 1839. Hamlin forwarded it to Governor Fairfield and his council the same day. In his covering letter, Hamlin stated that "extraordinary depredations are being committed on the public lands situated on these rivers, and that energetic measures will be required to arrest them." He went on to recommend that an armed party of at least fifty men would be required. Thus, Hamlin, in his last act as land agent, gave the new administration an opportunity to back its rhetoric with action. And it was not long in coming.

The next day, January 23, Fairfield forwarded the report to Maine's Senate and House of Representatives. After paraphrasing the report, Fairfield stated that revenue from the timber cut was worth roughly $100,000 in licencing fees alone, which, given the size of Maine's debt, was a considerable sum that could be added to the state treasury. Fairfield then said that, by the actions of the trespassers, "not merely the property, but the character of the State, is clearly involved." Further, the "Conduct so outrageous and high-handed as that exhibited by these reckless depredations upon the public property, calls for the most prompt and vigorous action of the Government." He then recommended that "the Land Agent be instructed forthwith to proceed to the place of operations on the Aroostook and also upon [the] Fish River, if practicable, with a sufficient number of men suitably equipped,

Governor John Fairfield of Maine, who initiated the Aroostook War by sending an armed posse into the Aroostook Valley in February 1839.

Engraving by Thomas Doney, Anthony, Edwards & Co.

to seize the teams and provisions, break up the camps, and disperse those who are engaged in this work of devastation and pillage." Fairfield urged confidentiality in this matter as he did not want to alert the trespassers. Because of this, it came to be reported that the matter had been discussed in "secret" sessions. On the same day, the legislature passed a Resolve "that the land agent be, and is hereby, authorized and required to employ forthwith sufficient force to arrest, detain and imprison all persons found trespassing on the territory of this State, as bounded and established by the Treaty of 1783" and authorized $10,000 to carry out the Resolve. The Senate endorsed the Resolve later in the day, and Fairfield approved it the next day.

It fell to the new land agent, Rufus McIntire, to enforce the Resolve. A political challenger for Fairfield's gubernatorial nomination, McIntire was a veteran of the War of 1812, an experienced lawyer and politician, and an anglophobe. As such, he was the right man for the job and could be counted on to see the mission through. He turned to Hastings Strickland,

Rufus McIntire, the Maine land agent who led the posse into the Aroostook Valley in February 1839.

Geo. H. Walker & Co., Boston

the sheriff of Penobscot County, to organize a posse, which would be armed as resistance was expected from the lumbermen. The posse of about two hundred men was organized into three groups — one each from Bangor, Oldtown, and Lincoln led by Captain Stover Rines, Captain William P. Parrott, and [Ward?] Witham, respectively. Accompanying the posse, in addition to McIntire, were two magistrates, Gustavus G. Cushman and Thomas Bartlett, whose role was to issue writs and initiate legal proceedings against the trespassers.

It became a popular belief that the posse consisted of either lumbermen or militiamen. Yet, although some might have been lumbermen and all would have been members of the Maine state militia, the posse was a civil, not a military, body. The source for the misunderstanding might be that most of the leaders also held militia rank — for example, McIntire was occasionally referred to as colonel and Sheriff Strickland was frequently referred to by his militia rank of major. Similarly, the presence of some lumbermen in its ranks probably led to the use of various names for the ensuing conflict now generally known as the Aroostook War: the "Lumbermen's War," the "Red Shirts War" — a reference to the shirts worn by many lumbermen — and the "Pork and Beans War," relating to the food the lumbermen ate. What the monikers all indicated, however, was the cause of the crisis: trespass timber.

Despite efforts to keep McIntire's mission a secret, word soon got out. On February 5, the Bangor *Daily Whig and Courier* announced that Sheriff Strickland had left that morning with a posse to remove the trespassers from the Disputed Territory. Proceeding north from Bangor along the Aroostook road to where it ended at Township No. 10, Masardis, the men and supplies travelled by sleigh. It could not have been a pleasant journey — the temperature in Bangor on February 7 was recorded as -24°F (-31 °C) — but surviving documents make no mention of hardships from the cold weather. In any case, the lumbermen in the posse would have been familiar with such conditions.

On the afternoon of February 8, the advance party of fifty men led by Captain Rines arrived at Masardis, with the rest of the posse expected to reach there the next day. Meanwhile, George W. Buckmore was sent to reconnoitre the situation. He travelled from Houlton to Woodstock, up the St. John, and then up the Aroostook to the rendezvous at Masardis. According to his report, he "apprehended that the trespassers would make trouble." Indeed, by February 7, rumours of the expedition had also reached New Brunswick, and expresses (messengers) were sent into the woods to advise the teams and men to withdraw.

As anticipated, the lumbermen and settlers along the Aroostook opposed the presence of the posse, but it is difficult to determine when the resistance began. Asa Dow, a farmer and lumberman from the Dumfries/Canterbury area south of Woodstock, had a number of crews cutting trespass timber along the Aroostook. When he heard about the posse, he discussed events with local settlers, who agreed that the posse had no right to be there. Dow reported that "the greater part of the settlers were intending to make Battle with them," The settlers assembled to oppose the posse, but when it did not appear they dispersed. It is not known what day this occurred, but it must have been prior to February 10.

Certainly, Governor Fairfield heard of local resistance. In a message to the House of Representatives on February 15, he reported that a group of about three hundred well-armed trespassers had attempted to stop the posse before it reached the Aroostook River. Upon seeing that the land agent had a brass 6-pounder cannon with him, they wisely withdrew. Curiously, this event is not mentioned in the Annual Report of the Land Agent, so it cannot be verified — indeed, local settlers recalled no confrontation with the posse at all.

Having regrouped at Masardis, on February 10 McIntire and the posse began moving down the Aroostook River toward what Maine called the East Line of the State (the Commissioners' Line), where they found evidence of abandoned timber operations but no men or teams. McIntire went ahead of the posse to Mr. Hooper's (Maysville, now part of Presque Isle) to explain his mission to the settlers there, who had been alarmed by the advance of the posse, and to reassure them. He encountered no hostility.

The next morning, February 11, Sheriff Strickland and the posse were about a mile above Hooper's when they came upon a line of fifteen or sixteen armed men guarding two horse teams that were trying to escape downriver. Strickland, in his sleigh with his driver, charged through the line — as he did so, one of the men fired at him, slightly wounding his horse — and pursued the teams for six or seven miles before catching them and bringing them back. The posse, following behind Strickland, captured the armed men, who now numbered about twenty with the addition of the teamsters. Strickland, assisted by magistrates Cushman and Bartlett, proceeded to hold court on the iced-over river. The charges related to the trespassing of foreigners on the public lands of Maine and to the "snapping of firearms" at, and the discharge of a musket toward, Strickland. Five men were sent to the Penobscot jail in Bangor; two others were arrested but released within a few hours. Peter Bull, who lived in the area, was also arrested, but released when Dennis Fairbanks and Colonel Ebenezer Webster posted his bail. The posse then continued down the Aroostook without further opposition until they reached the mouth of the Little Madawaska River at what is now Caribou.

Meanwhile, McIntire had taken the portage route that cut across a large loop in the Aroostook River and reached James Fitzherbert's house (now Fort Fairfield, Maine, about two miles west of the Commissioners' Line). There, McIntire expected to find an assembly of settlers to whom he intended to explain his mission. There was no gathering of the settlers and it appeared that all of the trespassers had fled across the Commissioners' Line into New Brunswick. McIntire returned to the posse's camp and made arrangements to have the seized timber marked. At this point, McIntire believed that his mission had been accomplished, and he began making arrangements to send the posse home, except for those men needed to secure the timber. He then travelled the six miles back to Fitzherbert's, accompanied by Cushman and Bartlett, where he was expecting to meet MacLauchlan, who was said to be *en route* at McIntire's invitation. Depending on the source, the meeting was to be either at Fitzherbert's or at Benjamin Tibbits's house in Tobique the following day. McIntire's motives for returning to Fitzherbert's were later challenged by his political opponents. They claimed that he left the safety of the posse's camp for the comfort of a feather bed; given that he was age fifty-five at the time, sleeping indoors instead of outdoors in a rough camp in sub-zero weather would have had its attractions. Regardless of the reason, it was a fateful decision.

In keeping with the custom of the time, many private homes were open to travellers who needed food and lodging, and Fitzherbert's was no exception. He had moved across the Commissioners' Line from New Brunswick and was operating a mill on a stream that entered the Aroostook River there. His house was quite a crowded place on the evening of February 12. In addition to McIntire's party, two other Americans, Colonel Ebenezer Webster and Captain John H. Pilsbury, were present, as were two New Brunswickers, or Provincials as they were known. They were Punderson Beardsley, a lumberman, and George Raymond, a teamster. Unbeknownst to the Americans, the lumbermen were aware of their movements. Beardsley had tried to enlist the aid of some aboriginal men, most likely Maliseet from the Tobique reserve, to scout for him. When they wisely declined to become involved, Beardsley placed several lumbermen as lookouts and to report on the posse's activities. Asa Dow had also been at Fitzherbert's, but he left that afternoon and had gone to Benjamin Tibbits's at Tobique, where a group of forty-six to fifty-eight lumbermen had gathered. They had decided that they needed to be better armed before acting against the posse, and by the time Dow arrived, they were fully armed. On February 11, "persons unknown" had broken into three militia arms stores in the Woodstock area and removed about a hundred "stand of arms"—a stand of arms consisting of musket, sling, bayonet and scabbard, ammunition box, and cross belts. Before the days of purpose-built armouries, it was customary to store arms at the homes of captains of the various militia companies.

Later in the day, Paul Beardsley left Tibbits's to see his brother, Punderson, and to get news of the posse's movements. Meanwhile, Punderson had been speaking with McIntire and Colonel Webster, who was also a well-known lumberman in the area. Both had said that they wanted to see MacLauchlan to make a proposal to him: they were prepared to release the seized timber provided the Maine land agent was paid 5 shillings per ton. Webster also told Beardsley that the posse had two brass cannon. When speaking with Raymond, Webster also claimed that all the settlers along the Aroostook were to become American citizens. Those who cooperated would be treated well, while those who resisted would be punished. This constituted a unilateral extension of US sovereignty into the Disputed Territory, similar to what the British had done in the northern portion. The key difference was that, whereas there were virtually no Americans in the northern portion, the Aroostook Valley had already been settled largely by British subjects. Moreover, the area was fully integrated into the New Brunswick economy. Under those circumstances there was bound to be some resistance to the posse.

The Beardsley brothers met, and Paul returned to Tibbits's with the news that the five Americans were at Fitzherbert's and that the rest of the posse was six miles away at the mouth of the Little Madawaska. On hearing this news, Dow ordered two teams of horses harnessed, and he set out for Fitzherbert's in two sleighs with fifteen or eighteen men armed

Sir John Harvey, lieutenant-governor of New Brunswick, initially took a firm stance in his dealings with Maine over the border controversy. He became indecisive after the Aroostook War ended in late March 1839 and the focus of the controversy shifted to the Madawaska settlement, resulting in his dismissal from office in 1841. NBM W701(1)

with muskets and rifles loaded with powder and ball and with bayonets fixed; they were fully prepared for any confrontation.

Fortunately, events unfolded peacefully. The lumbermen arrived at Fitzherbert's about midnight, surrounded the house, and arrested the Americans. Webster challenged Punderson Beardsley's authority to take him prisoner, to which Beardsley replied, by referring to the gun in his hand, "That is my authority." All five Americans were then taken to Tibbits's, where they spent the rest of the night. When they were searched, Cushman was found to have a pocket pistol and McIntire a pocket carbine. The next day, they were taken to James Jones's house at Wakefield, twelve miles above Woodstock. Dow left them there and proceeded to Woodstock with the intention of reporting his actions to the magistrates. While *en route*, he encountered Captain William Hawkshaw, Royal Engineers, and Acting Assistant Quartermaster-General of New Brunswick. Sir John Harvey had heard the rumours of the arrival of the posse in the Disputed Territory, and normally he would have relied on MacLauchlan to inform him of the situation. MacLauchlan, however, was in the Madawaska settlement, where he was helping to settle the accounts for the recent passage of troops to the Canadas. He was also investigating reports of distress and hardship among the Maliseet and the settlers there. Harvey, anxious to know what was happening, dispatched Hawkshaw to investigate.

Hawkshaw and Dow returned to Jones's, where the American prisoners were interviewed. McIntire confirmed his mission was to drive off the trespassers and, thinking that he had done this, was going to withdraw most of the posse on the fifteenth. He also stated that he had not intended to go to either the Fish River or the Madawaska settlement as he believed that MacLauchlan had suppressed trespass cutting in those areas. This was one of the matters that he wanted to discuss with MacLauchlan. As some point, Webster and Pilsbury convinced Dow that they were not with the posse. Rather, both being lumbermen, they were in the process of building a timber boom across the mouth of the Aroostook River. They also had a barrel of powder stored at Fitzherbert's that they were going to use to blow up a rock at the Aroostook Falls that was impeding the passage of timber. This, they said, was their reason for being at Fitzherbert's. Consequently, Dow released Webster and Pilsbury. After the meeting, Hawkshaw proceeded up the Aroostook and visited the site of the posse's camp, where he found evidence of a hasty departure, including a number of abandoned sleighs.

In fact, when word of the capture of McIntire and his party reached the posse, it had retreated, somewhat precipitously, to the camp at Masardis. The lumbermen had planted the rumour that a force of "300 White men and 25 Indians, well-armed" were coming to attack them. Another version of this story had "175 volunteers...and 25 Indians" on their way to disperse the posse. This had the desired effect of preventing the posse from pursuing the lumbermen into New Brunswick. Captain Stover Rines had been left in charge of the posse and was busily building fortifications at the camp in anticipation of an attack by the British. Strickland then rode one hundred and sixty miles in less than two days to Bangor—a ride that was to become famous—to bring news of the capture of McIntire and his party and the rumour of the advance of the British force. He then proceeded to

Augusta, the state capital, to inform Governor Fairfield of these events. Strickland was both praised and damned for this ride. While applauded by his supporters, which included Fairfield and land agent McIntire, for making a difficult ride to bring word of the capture, his opponents criticized him, believing his ride had been too precipitous. The *Bangor Whig*, though supporting the expedition, delighted in criticizing Strickland's dash. Their entry for February 15 was, "Mr. Sheriff Strickland arrived in this city about 4 o'clock yesterday afternoon having travelled 160 miles between that time and 12 o'clock the day before. This is certainly extraordinary speed, considering the flight was in the woods, but there is no calculating a man's velocity when he's *skeert!*" The episode also gave rise to a little ditty: "Run, Strickland, run!/ Fire, Stover, fire!/ Were the last words of McIntire."

Meanwhile, Asa Dow and the three remaining prisoners had reached Woodstock, where Dow laid his case before magistrates Richard Ketchum, J. Pearce, and John Diblee. There was much excitement in the town, and armed guards were placed around the prisoners' quarters. Major R.M. Kirby, commanding officer of the US Army detachment at Hancock Barracks in Houlton, tried to see them but was refused. On February 14, the magistrates sent the three Americans under the guard of Captain Elisha A. Cunliffe of the 1st Battalion, Carleton County militia, and four men, to Fredericton, where they were placed "under a charge of overt Acts of Jurisdiction over and Interference with the Disputed Territory." The next day, Punderson Beardsley and George Raymond arrived at Woodstock and gave depositions that implicated Webster as a "Principle in the American armed party." As Webster was on his way to Fredericton on business, word was sent to arrest him when he arrived. In their letter of February 15, the magistrates also reported that all of the militia arms had been returned. Also captured were two kegs of powder, three horses with harness, and three sleighs, and the magistrates asked for Harvey's direction as to their disposition.

The drama would have another odd twist. On February 13, MacLauchlan arrived at Tibbits's and was informed of the recent events. He then sent a report in a letter to Harvey and, accompanied by Captain Benjamin Tibbits of the Carleton County militia and another man, set out up the Aroostook to find the posse. His goal was to find out its intentions and to defuse the crisis if he could. When they arrived at Masardis, MacLauchlan met with Rines and warned him to disperse his party, as they had no authority to exercise jurisdiction within the Disputed Territory. After consulting with his officers, however, Rines arrested MacLauchlan, apparently in reprisal for the arrest of McIntire and his party. MacLauchlan explained to Rines that McIntire's capture had not been on the authority of the New Brunswick government, nor were the settlers at Tobique involved. He also tried to assure Rines that no force was on its way to attack the posse. This was to no avail, and on February 15 MacLauchlan and Tibbits were sent to Bangor, where they arrived on the seventeenth. The third man was detained for a time and then released.

A strange calm now descended over the Aroostook Valley. The land agent of Maine was under arrest in Fredericton, while the warden of the Disputed Territory was being detained in Bangor. Some controversy arose about this, as the Americans initially enjoyed the spartan conditions of the county jail while MacLauchlan was lodged in one of the better hotels in Bangor. The Americans were soon released, however, and took up commercial accommodations.

The lumbermen had succeeded—by fright alone—in their goal of removing the posse from the Aroostook Valley. But the posse had also achieved its goal: the lumbermen had been driven out of the Aroostook Valley and the cutting of trespass timber stopped. McIntire's and Webster's offers to let the timber leave the Aroostook if the Maine land agent were paid 5 shillings per ton seemed to reinforce the idea that the crisis was precipitated by Maine's need for money. Later in 1839, Massachusetts land agent George W. Coffin investigated the events of the Aroostook War and thought that Buckmore's estimates of the amount of trespass cutting had been greatly exaggerated. By his calculations, only about 8,000 tons of timber was cut in the Aroostook Valley in the winter of 1838/1839. This again reinforced the argument that Maine's need for money was the root cause of the Aroostook War.

In retrospect, it would appear that the Lumbermen's Resistance won the first skirmish but lost the war. If McIntire is to be believed, the posse's sweep through the Aroostook Valley ended on about February 15 and it then would have returned to Bangor. If so, the ensuing border crisis might not have happened at all. Instead, the focus of activity now shifted to Fredericton and Augusta, where events would escalate what started as a civil sweep through the Aroostook Valley to prevent the illegal cutting of timber into a full-blown border crisis that threatened to spark a third Anglo-American war.

Chapter Four

On the Brink of War

Mr. President, if you want war, I need only to look on in silence. The Maine people will make it for you, fast and hot enough; I know them. But if peace be your wish, I can give no assurance of success. The difficulties in its way will be formidable.

—General Winfield Scott to President Martin Van
Buren, February 28, 1839

In February 1839, as Asa Dow brought his five American prisoners to Woodstock and Captain Hawkshaw travelled upriver to investigate the rumours of an American invasion, Sir John Harvey, the lieutenant-governor of New Brunswick, faced a potentially serious crisis, but had little or no firm information on which to base his actions. On February 13, he issued an unusual proclamation:

Fredericton, 13th February, 1839

A PROCLAMATION

Whereas I have received information that a party of armed persons to the number of two hundred or more have invaded a portion of this province under the jurisdiction of Her Majesty's Government, from the neighbouring State of Maine, for the professed object of exercising authority, and driving off persons stated to be cutting timber therein; and that divers other persons have, without any legal authority, taken up arms with the intention of resisting such invasion and outrage, and have broken open certain Stores in Woodstock, in which arms and ammunition belonging to Her Majesty were deposited, and have taken the same away for the purpose,—I do hereby charge and command all persons concerned in such illegal acts forthwith to return the arms and ammunition illegally taken, to their place of deposit; as the Government of the province will take care to adopt all necessary measures from resisting any hostile invasion or outrage that may be attempted upon any part of Her Majesty's territories or subjects. And I do hereby charge and command all Magistrates, Sheriffs, and other Officers, to be vigilant, aiding and assisting in the apprehension of all Persons so offending, and to bring them to justice. And in order to aid and assist the Civil Power in that respect, if necessary, I have ordered sufficient Military Force to proceed forthwith to the place where these Outrages are represented to have been committed, as well to repel Foreign invasion, as to prevent the illegal assumption of Arms by Her Majesty's subjects in this Province. And further, in order to be prepared, if necessary, to call in aid of the Constitutional Militia Forces of the country, I do hereby charge and command the Officers commanding the first, and second Battalions of the Militia of the County of Carleton, forthwith to proceed, as the law directs, to the drafting of a body of men, to consist of one-fourth of the strength of each of those battalions, to be in readiness for actual service, should occasion require.

Facing Page: The response by Governor Fairfield of Maine to this proclamation escalated the border crisis from a civil to a military affair that became known as the Aroostook War. Maine Historical Society

ROYAL GAZETTE EXTRA.

FREDERICTON, 13th February, 1839.

 By His Excellency Major General Sir John Harvey, K. C. B. and K. C. H. Lieutenant Governor and Commander in Chief of the Province of New Brunswick, &c.   &c.   &c.

JOHN HARVEY.

A PROCLAMATION.

WHEREAS, I have received information that a party of armed persons, to the number of two hundred, or more, have invaded a portion of this Province, under the jurisdiction of Her Majesty's Government, from the neighbouring State of Maine, for the professed object of exercising authority, and driving off persons stated to be cutting Timber therein ; and that divers other persons have without any legal authority, taken up arms with the intention of resisting such invasion and outrage, and have broken open certain Stores in Woodstock, in which Arms and Ammunition belonging to Her Majesty were deposited, and have taken the same away for that purpose,—I do hereby charge and command all persons concerned in such illegal acts, forthwith to return the Arms and Ammunition, so illegally taken, to their place of deposit, as the Government of the Province will take care to adopt all necessary measures for resisting any hostile invasion or outrage that may be attempted upon any part of Her Majesty's Territories or Subjects.   And I do hereby charge and command all Magistrates, Sheriffs, and other Officers, to be vigilant, aiding and assisting in the apprehension of all Persons so offending, and to bring them to justice.   And in order to aid and assist the Civil Power in that respect, if necessary, I have ordered a sufficient Military Force to proceed forthwith to the place where these Outrages are represented to have been committed, as well to repel Foreign invasion, as to prevent the illegal assumption of Arms by Her Majesty's Subjects in this Province.   And further, in order to be prepared, if necessary, to call in the aid of the Constitutional Militia Force of the country, I do hereby charge and command the Officers commanding the first and second Battalions of the Militia of the County of Carleton, forthwith to proceed as the Law directs, to the drafting of a body of men, to consist of one fourth of the strength of each of those Battalions, to be in readiness for actual service, should occasion require.

Given under my Hand and Seal at Fredericton, the thirteenth day of February, in the year of our Lord one thousand eight hundred and thirty nine, and in the second year of Her Majesty's Reign.

By His Excellency's Command,

WM. F. ODELL.

GOD SAVE THE QUEEN.

Lieutenant-Colonel A.M.
Maxwell, commander of the
British regulars and New
Brunswick militia during the
Aroostook War. Col. Montgomery
Maxwell, *My Adventures*, Vol. 1 (London: Henry
Colburn, 1845)

The proclamation addressed all of the important points. Harvey made
it perfectly clear that the issue of control over the southern portion of the
Disputed Territory had not been resolved—in fact, he stated plainly that
a "portion of this province" had been invaded by a foreign power. He
provided firm direction that the provincial government would handle the
matter and that there was no need to take vigilante action. Furthermore,
the arms and ammunition had to be returned. Finally, he reassured New
Brunswickers by stating that a military force had been despatched and
that the militia battalions in the area were on standby to provide further
assistance. In case Governor Fairfield was not aware of this proclamation,
David M. Coffin of Spring Hill, New Brunswick, sent him a copy on
February 18.

Nevertheless, loyalties were not clear cut, and many of the persons on
both sides of the Commissioners' Line in the border crisis wanted it to end
so they could return to their business of cutting timber, with or without a

licence. Although Maine had precipitated the crisis by sending a heavily armed civilian posse into the Aroostook watershed, Governor Harvey's response was to send in the military. His purpose in doing so was probably as much to maintain civil order in New Brunswick as to guard Britain's sovereign interests along the border. The theft of military weapons was vigilante justice and was intolerable. Moreover, there was only so much that the local militia, as part of the community, could be expected to do. Even more crucially, Maine's action in the depths of winter highlighted the vulnerability of the only winter route to the Canadas. Harvey needed professional soldiers, and he sent them in.

The 36th (Herefordshire) Regiment of Foot had arrived in New Brunswick in January 1839 as the garrison regiment. Its commanding officer, Lieutenant-Colonel Archibald Montgomery Maxwell, led the military force to the disputed border area. It speaks to the enduring British view of the issue that Maxwell supposed that Maine's intentions were "to cut off our communications with Canada." In mid-February, he left for Woodstock with the provincial solicitor-general, George Frederick Street, as his legal advisor. He intended to go to the Madawaska settlement, but he found the excitement in Woodstock so great that he established his headquarters there. Harvey's orders were "to take command on the disputed frontier; with power to call out an additional militia force, to put the frontier in a state of defence, and at the same time to keep open our communication with Lower Canada: but to avoid, if possible, hostile collision." On the fifteenth, the Light Company of the 36th, accompanied by a detachment of the Royal Artillery, left Fredericton by sleigh. Further troop deployments followed soon afterward.

Having addressed the military situation, Harvey then turned to the diplomatic one. In a letter to Governor Fairfield dated February 13, he expressed his regret that Maine had sent an armed force into the Disputed Territory without prior notice. He went on to reiterate Britain's claim to exercise exclusive jurisdiction in the Disputed Territory pending the resolution of the boundary question and requested Fairfield to withdraw his force. If this did not happen, then Harvey was prepared to use military force to support Her Majesty's authority within the Territory and to protect its inhabitants. In an effort to appease Maine on the issue of illegally cut timber, Harvey wrote that he had given instructions for a boom to be placed across the mouth of the Aroostook River and that a seizing officer, supported by a guard, would prevent the passage of trespass timber into the St. John. Moreover, such timber would be seized and sold at public auction, with the proceeds being placed in the Disputed Territory Fund. In a twist of fate, the boom appears to have been the same one that Webster and Pilsbury had been constructing.

While this letter was being carried to Fairfield by a special messenger, Richard English, Fairfield also despatched a letter to Harvey by his special messenger, Jonathan P. Rogers. Fairfield asked if the "high-handed proceedings of the trespassers" were authorized by the provincial government, and he wanted McIntire and his party released. In the meantime, on February 15, Fairfield briefed his government about the situation and recommended the appointment of a temporary land agent and the raising of three hundred men to augment the agent's force. On the eighteenth, Fairfield updated his government, having now received Harvey's letter and a copy of the lieutenant-governor's proclamation. This information created great excitement in Augusta, especially Harvey's threat to use force to repel the land agent's party. Neither Fairfield nor his government were inclined to compromise; they believed they were clearly in the right and intended to stay the course. To that end, on February 20, the state passed a resolve endorsing any actions Fairfield might take to protect the timber of the state and authorizing "that a sufficient military force be forthwith stationed on the Aroostook River, west of the boundary-line of the State, as established by the Treaty of 1783; and on the river St. John, if found practicable." To that end, Maine was willing to spend $800,000, a significant undertaking for a state that was close to bankruptcy. The resolve also confirmed Maine's intention to take control of the Aroostook Valley and part of the St. John River area and keep it, despite any legal considerations in international law or problems of Anglo-American relations. Maine was claiming what it believed to be its inheritance from the 1783 Treaty of Paris.

On February 15, Fairfield appointed as interim land agent Charles Jarvis, who immediately set off for the posse's camp. On his way, he stopped

Major-General Isaac
Hodsdon, commander of
the Maine militia in the
Disputed Territory during
the Aroostook War.

History of Penobscot County, Maine (Cleveland:
Williams, Chase & Co., 1882)

to consult with Strickland. There was no difficulty finding reinforcements
for the posse. As Fairfield wrote, "indeed, it was hard work to hold volunteers back for thousands and thousands would have gone if permitted."
Although the numbers might have been a slight exaggeration, the eagerness
of the citizens of Maine to defend their state against the perceived injustices
and false claims of Britain was sincere. At the time, a great deal of anti-
British sentiment existed in Maine, particularly over the memory of British
occupations during the American Revolutionary War and the War of 1812,
as well as frustration over Britain's efforts to block Maine from its perceived
rightful ownership of all of the Disputed Territory.

Based on the support of the Maine Senate and House of Representatives, Fairfield sent a reinforcement of between four and five hundred men
to join the land agent's party. Two days earlier, on the sixteenth, he had
issued [Militia] General Order No. 5, commanding Major-General Isaac
Hodsdon of the Third Division of the Maine Militia to detach a draft of

a thousand men with officers and equipment. They were to "rendezvous at Bangor and proceed at the earliest possible moment" to join the land agent and to support him in carrying out the state's resolve of January 24 concerning the removal of trespassers from the public lands. General Order No. 6, issued on February 17, directed that the force was to be composed of infantry, light infantry, and riflemen, as well as one hundred and fifty artillerymen. They were to appear in Bangor by February 21 with their arms, equipment, and three days' provisions. Additional military stores were to be requisitioned from the quartermaster-general. The militiamen were "to serve for three months unless sooner discharged." The governor then requested and received authority to call up another ten thousand militia, to be drafted under authority of General Order No. 7, dated February 19, and to hold themselves "in readiness for active service." Fairfield did not know what the British response would be, but he clearly was preparing for war. He also sent a messenger to Major R.M. Kirby, commanding the two companies of the 1st Artillery that formed the garrison at Hancock Barracks in Houlton, asking for his assistance in "repelling an invasion of our territory." Kirby, however, wisely kept his garrison removed from Maine's activities, believing it was his duty not to involve the US government in a question of jurisdiction without having received specific orders from Washington. Kirby reportedly even denied the militia's request to borrow an American flag. Instead, Kirby confined his cooperation to intelligence gathering, reporting that a company of the British 36th Regiment had passed through Woodstock on February 16 *en route* to the Mouth of the Aroostook River and that another company had followed on the eighteenth under the command of Colonel Maxwell. He also noted that there was a rumour that reinforcements were expected from both the Canadas and the West Indies.

Meanwhile, Harvey and Fairfield continued to exchange letters. In one dated February 19, Fairfield defended his actions and explained that the "proceedings of our land agent were in execution of a Resolve of the Legislature of this State, adopted in *secret session*; and that no notice of these proceedings could have been given without an unqualified breach of faith and duty." He also challenged Britain's claim to have an agreement with the United States to exercise "exclusive possession and jurisdiction of" the Disputed Territory until the boundary was settled. This letter crossed Harvey's of February 18 that was in reply to Fairfield's of the fifteenth. Harvey advised that he had released McIntire and his party, who were free to return to Maine, but if friendly relations were to be maintained between Britain and the United States, Maine would have to withdraw its force, otherwise Harvey would "take military occupation of that territory." Also, any prisoners taken by Maine, including MacLauchlan, had to be turned over to the British authorities for trial. Finally, Harvey assured Fairfield that he would adopt "the strongest and most effectual measures" to stop and prevent any further trespass cutting.

Meanwhile, the New Brunswick solicitor-general, George F. Street, was at the Mouth of the Aroostook River. On February 17, he sent a letter to Jarvis, Maine's acting land agent, demanding that he and his posse withdraw from the Disputed Territory. The letter found Jarvis at Masardis. In his reply, Jarvis stated that he was in the state of Maine and that he would not leave unless directed to do so by the executive of his state; further, although he would regret the occurrence of any conflict, he would defend himself if attacked. The situation clearly had reached an impasse. Harvey, acting in accordance with the instructions of the British government, claimed exclusive jurisdiction over the Disputed Territory, while Maine argued that the Disputed Territory was and always had been part of Maine.

At Masardis, Jarvis quickly took charge of his civil force. When he arrived on the seventeenth, he found them busily fortifying the camp. Not all of the volunteers were keen to continue, and twenty-two were discharged. The rest, however, were in good spirits and ready for any task that awaited them. But besides the brass cannon, Jarvis had only one hundred muskets, so, following Fairfield's instructions, he waited for reinforcements. After a few difficulties with the militia authorities, Strickland had succeeded in obtaining arms from the Maine militia stores, and now about six hundred men, with provisions, equipment, and ammunition, were on the march and were expected to arrive at Masardis on the twentieth. Once reinforced, Jarvis proposed to advance down the Aroostook and set up a forward base near Beaver Brook, "unless previously occupied by Sir John." He was still concerned that the British would advance to force the land agent's posse from the Disputed Territory.

With the arrival of reinforcements and a sizable force now at his disposal, Jarvis detached a party of about one hundred men to carry out the second part of his mandate—to prevent trespassing on the Upper St. John. The party, led by Captain Alvin Nye and guided by George W. Buckmore, had a difficult trip through the woods to Fish River. On their arrival, they found lumbermen at work and proceeded to close down their operations. They arrested eleven men but released five and brought back only four to the camp. By February 22, Nye and his force had returned to Masardis. Once back, members of the posse took pity on the lumbermen, whose poverty was obvious, and collected $12 for them. They were then released after giving their word not to cut trespass timber again.

News of this raid soon reached the British authorities. On February 25, Captain Francis Rice of the Madawaska militia reported it to Captain Trollope at Andover. Rice proceeded to Woodstock to brief the 36th Regiment's commander, Colonel Maxwell, then went on to Fredericton to report to Harvey. It appears, however, that the British overlooked the significance of the raid. In the resolve of February 20, Maine had included the St. John River in its area of interest, and Nye's expedition had confirmed this claim. As well, the text of the resolve had been published in the Maine newspapers, and so the British should have been aware of it. In the following months, this failure to understand Maine's intentions would take on major importance.

While the war of words between Fredericton and Augusta continued, so too did the movement of troops. General Hodsdon's militia force having mustered in Bangor, on February 21 it began leaving for the Aroostook. Among the ten companies in the force were the Bangor Rifle Corps, the Bluehill Light Infantry, the Dexter Rifle Company, and the Castine Light Infantry. By the twenty-second, Oliver Frost, one of Hodsdon's aides-de-camp, had reached Masardis with the advance party. By this time, Jarvis had established an advance post along the Aroostook River, about four miles above Presque Isle, and was cautiously feeling his way down the river, still expecting to be opposed by the British. His next move would be an advance through Presque Isle, across the portage, and then up to the future site of Fort Fairfield. There had been a report about a British officer seen along the river who was believed to be carrying out a reconnaissance for possible defensive positions. The officer might have been Captain Hawkshaw, who was scouting in the area. Jarvis sent Captain Dennis Fairbanks back to Hodsdon suggesting that, instead of joining him at Masardis, he take his force to Houlton and then proceed north to the Aroostook River. This would serve to distract the British force at Woodstock and mask Jarvis's advance. Hodsdon quickly agreed, and ordered his force to change its line of advance. This new direction drew criticism from the Adjutant-General's Office, however, which reminded Hodsdon that, while he was to support Jarvis and work in cooperation with him, he was not "under the immediate orders of that officer" — clear evidence of a degree of friction between the land agent and the Adjutant-General's Office that would surface on other occasions and make the land agent's task more difficult. Later, a "man from Houlton" crossed the border and reported to the 36th's Colonel Maxwell that the first half of Hodsdon's force had arrived there on February 27 and that the remainder were due the next day. While this was happening, Elijah L. Hamlin, now the superintendent, Cavalry Corps of Videttes, was establishing a line of videttes — cavalrymen stationed in pairs every ten miles apart — to carry messages quickly between Bangor and Houlton.

The British were making similar deployments on the New Brunswick side of the Commissioners' Line. By February 16, Captain Nugent was at Tibbits's in Andover with his company of the 36th, and Captain Wyatt was at Dingee's near Buttermilk Creek (present-day Florenceville-Bristol). The militia drafts were also proceeding well. When the draft was held at Richmond Corner, all four companies had volunteered *en masse*. Spirits were high, and the men were looking for an adventure to enliven an otherwise dreary winter. On February 23, Colonel Maxwell issued a Militia General Order calling up or embodying three hundred militiamen from the 1st and 2nd Battalions of the Carleton County militia. Three companies of the 1st Battalion were to be stationed as follows: Captain Thomas G. Cunliffe's

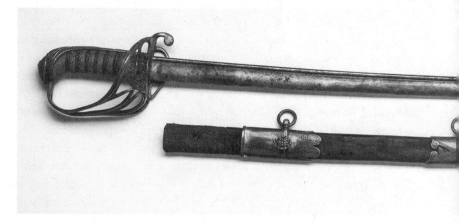

Sword belonging to Captain Charles McLauchlan, commander of the company of the 2nd Battalion, Carleton County Militia, posted at Grand Falls. McLauchlan, a veteran of the 104th (New Brunswick) Regiment of Foot, had received a land grant in the military settlement between the Presque Isle military post and Grand Falls. The Pattern 1822 Infantry Officers' sword, likely made between 1827 and 1830, bears the cipher of King George IV. With permission of McLauchlan's descendants

in Woodstock, Captain James Ketchum's in Hardscrabble, and Captain William McKenzie's at Richmond Corner. The two companies of the 2nd Battalion, commanded by Major A.B. Walsh, the acting commanding officer, were to deploy as directed by Captain Nugent at Andover. Each battalion draft was to include ten good men to act as axemen or pioneers. The embodied companies of the 2nd Battalion were destined for Grand Falls and Andover under Captains Charles McLauchlan and Murphy Giberson, respectively. Their movement was delayed, however, because their arms and ammunition had not arrived and the commissariat's arrangements for blankets and rations were incomplete. While they waited, the militia at Buttermilk Creek were drilled by a sergeant of the 36th. By February 26, Captain Trollope and his company were in Grand Falls, while Captain Nugent was at Andover and the Mouth of the Aroostook. Maxwell meanwhile sent a detachment of artillery and a 6-pounder gun

to Trollope. As well, one hundred stand of arms for the militia were to be forwarded to Andover and Grand Falls, with fifty stored at each location.

Maxwell was satisfied with the deployment. Militia drills were going well and the men showed enthusiasm for the possible task ahead. His philosophy was that they "must act purely on the defensive...but be prepared to resist aggression." As February drew to a close, Maxwell began to wonder if he should also start making plans to repel any intruders in the area of the Madawaska settlement. If so, he would need reinforcements, preferably British regulars. Fortunately, help was on its way.

While Maxwell was coordinating the call-up of the Carleton County militia, George Shaw, the adjutant-general of militia in Fredericton, was doing the same for the rest of the provincial militia. On February 19, drafting and embodiment were ordered for various dates until mid-March. Table 1 provides a summary of this activity. The drafts of the York County militia were formed into a battalion under the command of Lieutenant-Colonel John Robinson. Similarly, the Carleton militia drafts were formed into a battalion under Lieutenant-Colonel John Allen. There was an outpouring of enthusiasm, and non-drafted militia men were allowed to serve as volunteers in place of the drafted men. Vacancies in existing militia units were filled and new ones, such as the City Guard of Saint John, were formed to accommodate the overflow. The Provincial

Table 1: Drafting and Embodiment of New Brunswick Militia, 1839

Unit	Number	Captains	Location
1st, 2nd, and 3rd Battalions, York Militia	300	D.L. Robinson George Clements George Long John McGibbon John Yerxa	Fredericton area
1st Battalion, Saint John Militia	75	Charles Drury	Saint John
City Rifle Battalion, Saint John	75	T.B. Millidge	Saint John
1st Battalion, Charlotte County	50	James Boyd	St. Andrews
2nd Battalion, Charlotte County	50	Thomas Mitchell	St. Stephen
New Brunswick Regiment of Artillery[a]	20		Fredericton
	34		Woodstock
	40[b]		Saint John
	15		St. Andrews
Troops of cavalry from Woodstock, Fredericton, and probably Saint John			Along the line of communications from Grand Falls, later Madawaska, to Saint John

[a] Including two light 3-pounder guns.
[b] Plus the adjutant.

Militia Act was amended to allow the formation of additional companies of dragoons and riflemen. In early March, the Carleton Light Dragoons and the Woodstock Rifle Company under Captain Rufus S. Demill joined Maxwell's force. The role of the embodied militia, outside of Carleton County, was primarily to back-fill the regular troops who had gone to the frontier and "to protect public and private property."

Similar drafts and call-outs were taking place in Maine. On February 22, a force of about eight hundred and fifty men from the 1st Brigade of the Second Division was ordered to muster at Augusta under the command of Brigadier-General George W. Bachelder. On the same day, Major-General Ezekiel Foster was ordered to muster 369 men of his division at Calais. Then, on February 27, the drafts from the Fifth Division were ordered to muster at Portland on March 4 and those of the Sixth Division at Augusta on March 6. The men of the Fifth and Sixth Divisions were not called forward to the frontier, however, and did not proceed beyond Augusta.

Harvey's initial instructions to Maxwell to remain on the defensive were endorsed by Sir John Colborne, the governor-general of British North America and, by practice, a major-general in the British army. British North America was divided into two military commands: Canada Command and Nova Scotia Command, which included New Brunswick. The senior military commander in Nova Scotia Command was Sir Colin Campbell, who was also the lieutenant-governor of that province. While Harvey, also a major-general, commanded in New Brunswick, he was subordinate to both Colborne and Campbell. Harvey had apprised Colborne of Maine's incursion in a letter dated February 12. Colborne's reply was prompt: although he endorsed Harvey's deployment of troops to the frontier as a show of force, he agreed that any attempt to drive the intruders out would "involve the two Countries in War." Harvey should attack, however, if Maine made any aggressive moves toward the "settled frontier." Colborne also alluded to the ongoing border friction between the Canadas and the northern states and was convinced that the US government would intervene "to check the infamous conduct of the Patriots and Brigands as far as they are allowed by their own ungovernable population." Many Americans living in border states such as Michigan, New York, and Vermont had been harbouring rebels fleeing the Canadas and aiding them in cross-border raids. Prophetically, Colborne suggested that, if Harvey succeeded in establishing a correspondence with Fairfield, he suggest "a conventional border line" as the solution to the border controversy; meanwhile, Campbell, Harvey's superior in Nova Scotia, ought to send reinforcements, and he soon sent them himself.

Given the presence of the Maine militia in Houlton and the armed posse, Harvey and Maxwell were concerned about an American move against either Woodstock or the Madawaska settlement. The 36th Regiment, which had arrived in New Brunswick only in January 1839, had been formed into six service companies with a total strength of five hundred and thirty men plus officers. One company was stationed in Saint John, another in Fredericton, and the rest were deploying to the frontier along with available members of the Royal Artillery, backfilled by the embodied companies of militia. In Halifax, Campbell, for his part, ordered the 69th (South Lincolnshire) Regiment of Foot under Lieutenant-Colonel Eaton Monins to sail from Barbados. The regiment began arriving in Saint John on March 4, and started moving forward once winter kit and transportation had been arranged. With the 69th on its way to Woodstock, Harvey wrote to Maxwell on March 6 that he soon "will have sufficient force to defend your position against all comers." Colborne, too, responded to Harvey's further request for reinforcements by ordering the 11th (North Devonshire) Regiment of Foot under Lieutenant-Colonel George L. Goldie to the Madawaska settlement. The regiment, in fact, had passed through New Brunswick the previous December, on its way to Lower Canada, and now had to retrace its steps. Leaving two companies in Chambly, near Montreal, where rebel activity was still a threat, the headquarters and one company remained at St. André, along the St. Lawrence River, while the remaining three companies, with a detachment of Royal Artillery armed with guns and rockets, marched to the Madawaska settlement, where Captain Hawkshaw and Assistant Deputy Commissary General William Milliken prepared for their arrival; the reinforcements seem to have been in place by March 11.

Mounting a winter campaign is never easy, and it was significantly more difficult in the early Victorian era. Normally, troops would go into winter quarters in the fall and wait for spring before renewing operations, but if there had to be a campaign in the Disputed Territory, winter was probably the best time to do it. Good transportation routes were needed to deploy troops. These existed in New Brunswick; a road ran as far upriver as Grand Falls and the frozen surface of the St. John River and its tributaries provided travel by sleigh, the preferred mode of transportation. The Americans also now had a good road, the Military Road, between Bangor and Houlton. Beyond that were only rough, winter roads that depended on frozen ground and snow cover and, of course, the surfaces of frozen lakes and rivers. Overall, the British had the transportation advantage. Deploying large numbers of troops also meant feeding and supplying them. The British already had members of the Commissariat Department in place and had recently made arrangements to move numbers of troops over the Grand Communications Route to the Canadas. Despite this expertise, there were delays in embodying elements of the militia, which could not be equipped and supplied as quickly as desired. In a letter dated March 4, Harvey acknowledged that the crisis had found them short of troops and supplies of all kinds. He nonetheless wrote to W.H. Robinson, the Assistant Commissary General in Charge, in appreciation of the efforts his department had made supporting the troops and militia during the winter.

The American system, in contrast, was organized on the fly, but seems to have been equally effective. The posse had been accompanied by supply wagons — likely with sled runners attached. The militia reported to its muster points with "three days' rations [and] suitable carriages, provisions, camp equipage and camp utensils." The Maine militia organized a system of commissaries and quartermasters to resupply the troops. Among them was Shepard Cary, a businessman and lumberman from Houlton, who already had held an appointment as sutler to Hancock Barracks. Upon his appointment as an assistant quartermaster, Cary was ordered to report to Houlton, where he would perform the duties of a quartermaster, a commissary, and a member of the Forage Masters Department. This was certainly a case of multitasking. The British also did their part to complicate Maine's logistics system. On March 9, Maxwell reported to Harvey that the detachment at Andover had blocked the Aroostook portage to stop supplies going from New Brunswick to the Americans at Fort Fairfield. The next day, Maxwell also stopped the cross-border movement of provisions from New Brunswick to Houlton. This, of course, forced the Maine militia and the land agent's posse to fall back on the longer and more difficult method of carrying supplies overland from Bangor.

As the forces deployed on both sides of the Commissioners' Line, the focus of the crisis shifted to Washington. Harvey had first informed Henry S. Fox, the British ambassador, of the developing crisis on February 13 and was providing him with frequent updates. Governor Fairfield, however, did not inform President Martin Van Buren of the crisis until February 18. In his letter, Fairfield outlined events to date, including the mobilization of the state militia, and requested Van Buren's support. The next day, Fairfield specifically asked for federal troops to assist him and that Major Kirby be ordered "to co-operate with the forces of this State in repelling an invasion of our territory."

On receiving Harvey's despatch, Ambassador Fox immediately wrote to the US Secretary of State, John Forsyth. Fox reiterated the British understanding that "all that part of the disputed territory is placed under the exclusive jurisdiction of Her Majesty's authority" and invoked "the immediate interference of the General Government of the United States, to prevent the threatened collision by causing Maine to withdraw voluntarily" its forces. Forsyth's reply came two days later and contained a bombshell: the US government denied that any such agreement about jurisdiction existed. This assertion was reaffirmed by a Resolution of the US Senate Committee on Foreign Relations dated February 28. In taking this stance, the Americans were strictly correct; the so-called understanding had not taken the form of a written agreement but had been developed through a series of exchanges of letters since 1818. Each side had placed their own interpretation on them. Things would have been much simpler if there had been a written agreement such as the Anglo-American Convention of 1818 that established joint jurisdiction over the Oregon Territory. But the understanding had never become that formal. As a result, both sides now operated on a set of assumptions that the other did not share.

By late winter 1839, the border crisis was threatening to escalate into the third Anglo-American war. The rhetoric became more heated, and neighbouring states and provinces became involved. On February 29, Nova Scotia offered to provide one-third of its militia, up to eight thousand men, to help defend against an American attack and voted £100,000 to pay for this force. The Quebec Volunteer Cavalry and the 3rd Provisional Battalion and the Cornwall Light Infantry from Upper Canada volunteered their services. On February 20, Governor Edward Everett of Massachusetts pledged his state's support for Maine should the government of the United States request it—a somewhat muted response since Massachusetts legally could not deploy its militia outside the state. Other states were also making unofficial offers of support. The situation was rapidly spinning out of control.

At this point, Major-General Winfield Scott, the commanding general of the Eastern Department of the US Army, who had been engaged in keeping the peace along the border between the Canadas and the northern states, entered the picture. The Canadian rebels who had fled to the United States after their failed rebellions had kept the border in a state of tension with help from American sympathizers, such as the Hunters' Lodges. Now Scott learned that a war might start in another part of his command. On February 23, he arrived in Washington and met with the secretary of war, Joel Roberts Poinsett, and President Van Buren. Van Buren did not want war with Britain, but neither could he refuse Maine's request for assistance. On March 3, while looking for a way to defuse the situation, Van Buren signed a Law for the Defence of the United States, which authorized him to employ the navy and army, as well as state militia and fifty thousand volunteers, should war break out, and a sum of $10,000,000 to pay for it. In the event of war, in fact, Van Buren would have had to depend on volunteers, since the US Army, less than 12,500 strong, was fully engaged in the Seminole War in Florida, the forced removal of the Cherokee to the west along the "trail of tears," and in trying to maintain peace along the northern border with the Canadas. The British, as a result of the rebellions of 1837 and 1838, had over 11,399 regulars in the Canadas plus 2,590 in Nova Scotia Command. The Royal Navy also ruled the waves. For Van Buren, then, this was no time for war with Britain, which he might have

Lieutenant-General Winfield Scott, President Martin Van Buren's
"troubleshooter" sent to resolve the border crisis.

Robert Walter Weir, Metropolitan Museum of Art

envisioned as a repeat of the War of 1812, when neither side had won the land war, but the Royal Navy had imposed a stranglehold on American commerce and driven the country to the brink of bankruptcy.

Fortunately, peace negotiations were also progressing well. On February 27, Ambassador Fox and Secretary of State Forsyth signed a memorandum that formed the basis for a new agreement about the Disputed Territory: New Brunswick would not expel Maine's forces in the Aroostook Valley, while Maine would voluntarily withdraw them from the bounds of the Territory. Any future operations to disperse trespassers would be "conducted by concert, jointly or separately" by Maine and New Brunswick. Basically, this would return the situation to the pre-crisis point, with the focus on the Aroostook River and no mention either of jurisdiction or of the Fish River. The two national governments would continue to work toward a solution to the border question. The next step was to obtain the concurrence of Maine and New Brunswick on the agreement.

The ensuing events highlighted the differences between the British and US forms of government. The foreign policy of British North America was controlled by London; lieutenant-governors, such as Harvey, served at Her Majesty's pleasure, and were tasked with enforcing instructions from the imperial government. Thus, on the British side, Viscount Palmerston at the Foreign Office endorsed the agreement in a letter dated April 6. In the United States, however, individual states were not subject to the same degree of central control. It would be necessary to sell the provisional agreement to Maine, and to this end President Van Buren turned to General Scott. During a meeting, most likely on February 28, this exchange took place:

> General Scott: "Mr. President, if you want *war*, I need only to look on in silence. The Maine people will make it for you, fast and hot enough; I know them. But if peace be your wish, I can give no assurance of success. The difficulties in its way will be formidable."

> "Peace with honor" was the reply from the President.

Bronze 6-pounder, Model 1838, in front of the library, Fort Fairfield, Maine, brought to the area by either the Maine militia or the land agent's posse. Cast by Cyrus Alger of Boston in 1839, it is typical of the cannon deployed by both sides during the Aroostook War. Photograph by the author

With that, Scott proceeded to Maine to convince Governor Fairfield to agree. *En route*, he stopped in Boston to discuss his mission with the Massachusetts governor and to elicit his support. On March 15, he reached Augusta.

As these events played out on the international stage, troops were on the move locally. Jarvis continued his cautious advance down the Aroostook River, fully expecting to be challenged by the British at any moment. On February 25, Lieutenant George W. Towle with seventy-one men moved from Masardis to the present site of Caribou, at the upper end of the portage. Having met no opposition, Jarvis joined Towle's party and advanced across the portage to what is now Fort Fairfield. By then, the posse could muster upwards of six hundred men in the area, and they started building huts for accommodation and field fortifications. They also made plans to build a timber boom across the Aroostook, which would allow the land agent to stop and sort legal timber from trespass timber when the river opened up in the spring. On the twenty-seventh, other elements of the posse joined them. By March 1, Jarvis was referring to his new post as Fort Fairfield.

The presence of the posse did not bode well for Fitzherbert. Jarvis was amused by the fact that Fitzherbert's house was in the line of fire should the posse's cannon be used against any invaders coming up the Tobique road from Andover. Jarvis also obtained testimony that Fitzherbert had been involved in McIntire's capture and, on March 3, had him arrested and taken to Lincoln for trial. The record is not clear, but it appears that the charges were quietly dropped. On March 7, McIntire arrived at Fort Fairfield to reassume his leadership of the posse, and Jarvis became an assistant land agent.

While Fox and Forsyth were drafting their agreement, Harvey and the Executive Council of New Brunswick still clung to the hope that the crisis could be defused if New Brunswick stepped up its efforts to prevent the cutting of trespass timber in the Disputed Territory. On February 27, they authorized Warden MacLauchlan "to proceed there and use the utmost vigilance to detect and prevent all Trespassers [from cutting timber]." He was to go via Houlton, show his orders to the officer in command of the American military force there, and ask for passes that would allow him to carry out his task without inference from any Maine forces in the area. In his letter of reply dated March 2, Hodsdon, in command of the Maine militia at Houlton, refused to recognize MacLauchlan's orders, as he was not allowed "to permit any forces, armed or unarmed, not of this State to exercise any jurisdiction or pre-eminence over that part of the State of Maine denominated 'The disputed Territory'." However, he graciously forwarded a copy of MacLauchlan's orders to Governor Fairfield for further comment.

It was during this time that the only "fighting" between the Maine militia and British regulars occurred. Fortunately, it was unofficial and the injuries minor in nature. Soon after their arrival at Houlton, about a half-dozen Maine militiamen, accompanied by two citizens of Houlton, crossed the Commissioners' Line and went a mile or two to Jones's Tavern (Richmond), where the British advanced post was located. The two sides intermingled and, depending on which version of the reports that appeared in the *Bangor Whig* one believes, words were spoken and a scuffle either did or did not occur. If it did, the worst injuries were a bloody nose or two. The Americans posted a guard on the border to prevent further occurrences.

Meanwhile, Colonel Maxwell in Woodstock and Major Kirby in Houlton maintained contact with each other, but their main concern was to develop procedures to prevent desertion. Soon after the British regulars arrived in Woodstock, three American soldiers deserted to them. A few nights later, there was an alarm as, in turn, some British soldiers tried to desert. This attempt seems to have been prevented, but American papers later reported that three British deserters had arrived in Bangor. So, despite the tensions created by the Aroostook War, the normal problems of armies persisted.

Meanwhile, Hodsdon, having received orders to position his force at Presque Isle (of the Aroostook), was preparing to advance from Houlton. Once there, he was to open a road to Masardis — as spring approached, the ice roads on the rivers would become unusable — to facilitate a link-up with Bachelder's force, which had left Bangor by March 11 and was proceeding north along the Aroostook road. As the first step in his advance, Hodsdon sent his engineer, Captain Henry E. Prentiss, to establish a forward post near where the Presque Isle (of the St. John) crossed the Commissioners' Line (near Bridgewater, Maine). The post was garrisoned by two companies, under the command of Lieutenant-Colonel George W. Cummings, who quickly built breastworks (or abattis) of fallen trees for their defence and huts for their accommodation. This turned out to be the closest point of contact between the forces of Maine and New Brunswick, with sentries from both sides positioned on opposite sides of a small hill. Fortunately, no collisions took place. On March 9, Hodsdon sent four of the remaining nine companies at Houlton forward to Presque Isle (of the Aroostook), their route roughly following present-day US Route 1 from Houlton to Mars Hill and then swinging northwest. While the remaining five companies were preparing to leave on March 11, they practised their marksmanship. One of their targets was an effigy of Queen Victoria. When he heard about this, Harvey lodged a protest with Hodsdon, who apologized for the poor manners of some of his troops.

As the militia was building up its strength in the Aroostook Valley, McIntire had planned to reduce the size of his posse, but he placed this move on hold while he tried to find out if the militia would be permitted to advance up to the Commissioners' Line at Fort Fairfield. Indeed, neither side really knew what the other was doing. The arrival of the 11th Regiment at Madawaska on March 9 created alarm at Fort Fairfield and, fearing an attack, McIntire requested the deployment of two militia companies to reinforce him. This answered the question of whether or not the militia could deploy along the frontier, and on March 13 the two companies from Presque Isle (of the St. John) arrived at Fort Fairfield. The same day, McIntire discharged two hundred members of his posse, retaining only those needed to work on building the boom, which had started on March 11 and was completed by April 3. At 447 yards long and anchored on seven piers, it would have been a formidable barrier to logs and log rafts coming down the Aroostook River in the spring.

On March 17, Hodsdon arrived at Fort Fairfield and established his headquarters there. Work continued on the defences, barracks, and the inevitable parade ground. The post was well supplied with artillery, having two 6-pounder and two 4-pounder field pieces. Meanwhile, Bachelder's men had started arriving at Machias about March 16. Their artillery consisted of two 4-pounder field guns. McIntire was concerned about a possible British advance from the Madawaska settlement up the Fish River and overland toward Masardis. Bachelder was to defend against this by guarding the Aroostook road from below Masardis and then around and down the Aroostook River to Presque Isle. This would also guard the rear of Hodsdon's militia further down the Aroostook and provide reinforcements if Fort Fairfield was attacked.

The British, too, were concerned about an attack, from Maine. Fearing a move through the woods to Fish River and then on to the Madawaska settlement, on March 11 Harvey wrote a letter to Lieutenant-Colonel Goldie at Madawaska advising him to remain on the left, or northern, bank of the St. John River and to fall back on Grand Falls if an attack took place. Soon afterwards, having learned that all of the 11th Regiment and its attachments had arrived, Harvey told Goldie to hold his ground if attacked, as he would be reinforced by the flank companies of the 36th Regiment at Grand Falls and Andover along with its two 6-pounder field pieces. Goldie could also deploy some of his troops on the right, or southern, bank of the river, which he did. They were quartered in Simon Hebert's house in present day-Madawaska, Maine. Harvey did not seem overly concerned about any American advance on Woodstock or Andover because Maine was only interested in the Disputed Territory and not in any area that was clearly recognized to be within the boundaries of New Brunswick, but he did send companies of the 69th Regiment to Woodstock to reinforce the garrison there.

Thus, at the height of the crisis, in mid-March 1839, troops were deployed along the border as follows (Table 2 presents a simple comparison of the approximate strengths):

St-André, Lower Canada: headquarters and one company of the 11th Regiment; two companies of the regiment were still in Chambly.

Madawaska: three companies of the 11th Regiment, a detachment of Royal Artillery (with a 6-pounder gun and rockets), and the Carleton Light Dragoons (couriers); two companies of the 11th, commanded by Lieutenant-Colonel Goldie, and one gun were located on the right, or south, bank of the St. John to reinforce Britain's claim of jurisdiction over all of the Madawaska settlement; the 3rd Battalion, Carleton Militia, based at the Madawaska settlement, was not embodied as it was feared their loyalty might have been compromised by American agitators.

Grand Falls: one company of the 36th Regiment, a detachment of Royal Artillery with a gun, and a company of the 2nd Battalion, Carleton Militia.

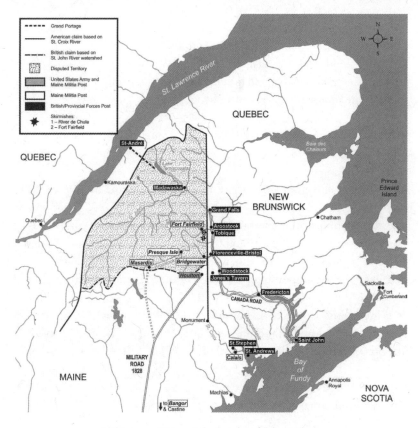

Military positions at the height of the crisis. MB

Tobique and the Mouth of the Aroostook: one company of the 36th Regiment, a detachment of Royal Artillery with a 6-pounder gun, and one company of the 2nd Battalion, Carleton Militia; there was an advanced post at the Falls of the Aroostook;

Fort Fairfield: nine companies of the 3rd Division, Maine militia, under Major-General Hodsdon, and approximately sixty members of the posse under Colonel Jarvis.

Presque Isle of the Aroostook: three companies of the 2nd Division and two companies of the 3rd Division, Maine militia.

Masardis: approximately three hundred men from the 2nd Division, Maine militia, under Brigadier-General Bachelder.

Florenceville-Bristol (Buttermilk Creek): a company of the 1st Battalion, Carleton Militia.

Bridgewater: two companies of the 3rd Division, Maine militia.

Woodstock: one company of the 36th Regiment and four companies of the 69th Regiment, a detachment of Royal Artillery with two 12-pounder howitzers and a 6-pounder gun, a detachment of New Brunswick Militia Artillery, three companies of the 1st Battalion, Carleton Militia, under Lieutenant-Colonel Allen, and the York Light Dragoons (couriers). There was an advanced post of seven men of the 69th Regiment at Richmond (Jones's tavern) on the Houlton Road. Lieutenant-Colonel Maxwell of the 36th Regiment commanded all the forces in and above Woodstock.

Houlton: three companies (120 men) of the 1st Regiment, US Artillery, and two companies of locally raised Maine militia.

Fredericton: two companies of the 36th Regiment, a detachment of Royal Artillery, rear parties of the 11th, 65th and 93rd Regiments, a Royal Engineer, a detachment of New Brunswick Militia Artillery, and three companies of the York Militia under Lieutenant-Colonel Robinson.

Saint John: one company each of the 36th and 69th Regiments, a detachment of Royal Artillery, rear parties of the 11th, 65th, and 93rd Regiments, a Royal Engineer, a detachment of New Brunswick Militia Artillery, and approximately three companies of the Saint John city Militia under Lieutenant-Colonel Peters.

Table 2: Approximate Strengths of British and US Forces in the Maine-New Brunswick Region, 1839

Type	Total		On the Frontier	
	British	US	British	US
Regular	1,398	120	956	120
Militia	950	2,904	433	1,618
Posse		750		60
Total	2,348	3,774	1,389	1,798

St. Stephen: one company of the 4th Battalion, Charlotte County Militia.

Calais: five companies of the 7th Division, Maine militia, under Major-General Foster.

St. Andrews: a detachment of Royal Artillery, a detachment of New Brunswick Militia Artillery, and one company of the 1st Battalion, Charlotte Country Militia.

Southern Maine: drafts from the 5th, 6th, and 8th Divisions, Maine militia, mustering at Portland, Augusta, and Skowhegan.

It is difficult to be more precise about the strengths of the posse and New Brunswick militia, which fluctuated, and because accurate records either were not kept or have not survived. There is a persistent belief that, because Fairfield warned ten thousand militiamen for duty, they were all mustered and all served in the Disputed Territory; in fact, the numbers probably never exceeded 1,618.

With troops deployed along the border and some in close contact with each other, it is not difficult to imagine that an incident might have occurred to spark a confrontation or even war. Now was the right time for General Scott to begin Van Buren's peace mission. A well-respected army officer and hero of the War of 1812, Scott was a good choice. If anyone could persuade Maine to accept the draft agreement, he was the one to do it. Scott also knew Harvey from the War of 1812 — both had served on the Niagara frontier and had met on several occasions under flags of truce. Following the American raid on York (Toronto) in late July 1813, Scott found and returned to Harvey a miniature portrait of his wife that had been looted by an American soldier. During the intervening years, the two had maintained a friendly correspondence. Their personal, cordial, shared experience of war and profession was instrumental in defusing the crisis.

When Scott arrived in Augusta about March 8, he found a city primed for war. His observations at the time give an excellent description of the political situation: "In the legislature, the weight of talent and information was with the Whig minority. Hence, they were much feared; for having recently been in power, the least error on the side of the Democrats might again give them the State. The popular cry being for war, the Whigs were unwilling to abandon that hobby-horse; but the Democrats were the first in that saddle and rode furiously." Scott, a Whig, first had to persuade both Democrats and Whigs to trust him. He then had to win them over to the draft agreement, a task he accomplished through skilful negotiations frequently conducted during friendly social interactions. Dealing with Harvey would be an easier task, as Harvey already had instructions from his superiors to cooperate in implementing the agreement.

By March 21, Scott had worked out an agreement acceptable to both Fairfield and Harvey. The essence of it was that, pending "the expected renewal of negotiations... on the subject of the said disputed territory":

> Harvey would not "seek to take military possession of that [disputed] territory, or to seek, by military force, to expel there from the armed civil *posse*, or the troops of Maine."

> In return for this undertaking, "it is not the intention of the Governor of Maine... to attempt to disturb by arms the said province, in the possession of the Madawaska Settlement, or to attempt to interrupt the usual communication between that Province and Her Majesty's upper Provinces."

Both Britain and Maine would hold possession of a part of the Disputed Territory in which the right to hold it was claimed by the other party.

If all was agreed to, the governor of Maine would "withdraw the military force of the State from the said disputed territory, leaving only, under a land agent, a small civil *posse*, armed or unarmed, to protect the timber recently cut, and to prevent further depredations."

Scott signed the agreement on March 21, followed by Harvey on March 23, and Fairfield on March 25. Maine was left in control of the Aroostook Valley while New Brunswick retained the rest of the Disputed Territory—at least that is how the British understood the agreement. The central fact, however, was that the Aroostook War was over, and it was time to start drawing down the troops along the border and in the Disputed Territory.

For a hasty campaign conducted during the depth of the cold winter months, there were surprisingly few casualties. The British records indicate that three soldiers died, but do not say how. Only one member of the posse was reported to have died and none of the militia. One militiaman had his toes amputated due to frostbite suffered while on the march from Bangor to Houlton. Indeed, the lack of adequate winter clothing was a problem for both sides. The British regulars were issued winter kit—items such as flannel shirts and drawers, fur caps with ear flaps, fur gloves or mitts, and snow boots or moccasins—that they paid for out of their wages. Many soldiers probably provided their own winter clothing when issue items were not available—many members of the New Brunswick militia apparently were reimbursed nine shillings for providing their own winter boots. On the other side, the *Bangor Whig* reporter in Houlton wrote on March 5 that the American soldiers were generally in good health considering "many of them in the hurry coming thinly clad, without the necessary clothing, shoes or blankets, to protect them from the unavoidable exposure of a winter campaign, in the want of suitable quarters, or the change from their usual diet at home to rations of hard bread and raw pork." Deficiencies in

British soldier in winter
dress, circa 1839.
LAC C-031249

winter clothing made finding shelter important. Existing buildings, such
as houses and barns, were used; otherwise, the soldiers quickly built huts
or other types of accommodation.

The end of March was an opportune time for the crisis to end. On
March 27, Hamlin had advised Fairfield that the line of vedettes between
Fort Fairfield and Houlton could not be maintained beyond mid-April,
when the winter road was expected to break up. Similarly, as it appeared
there would be a peaceful conclusion to the Aroostook War, Goldie in
Madawaska urged Harvey to allow him to return to St-André before the
winter road broke up. The withdrawal of the forces began immediately
upon Fairfield's consent to the agreement. General Order No. 29, dated
March 25, ordered Hodsdon "to make immediate preparation for retiring
with the troops of his command from the valley of the Aroostook"; he
would do so once the land agent had a "suitable civil force" in place "to
protect the timber and other public property." On April 5, Major-General

Foster's force at Calais was discharged and the additional drafts that were mustering were also ordered back to their homes.

A series of inspections accompanied by speeches congratulating the troops on their performance was a standard feature of these discharge parades. On March 27, Harvey travelled to Woodstock and held an inspection on the ice of the Meduxnakeag River, where the Royal Artillery, the 36th and 69th Regiments, the New Brunswick Militia Artillery, the 1st Carleton Battalion, the Woodstock Rifle Company, and the York Hussars were on parade. The next day, there was a levee, which Major Kirby and two other American officers attended. A District General Order dated March 27 thanked and dismissed the troops; the regulars returned to their peacetime stations and the militia to their homes. The next day, Maxwell issued a Militia District Order in which he singled out one company for praise: "the Borderers, commanded by a gallant old veteran — Captain M'Kenzie — the martial appearance of whose company was not to be wondered at, when was seen suspended at his breast the glorious trophy of his having fought on the immortal Field of Waterloo!"

The border crisis known as the Aroostook War had come to an end. It might well have ignited a war between Britain and the United States, but fiery hearts in Augusta and along the border had been overruled by cooler heads in Washington and London. The boundary dispute, however, was still not settled — despite the agreement signed by Scott, Harvey, and Fairfield, the region saw almost three more years of tension. Maine continued to move forward into the southern half; Britain pushed back, keen to protect its all-important lines of communication. With civil and military forces deployed along both sides of it, the fabled "Undefended Border" had not yet come into being.

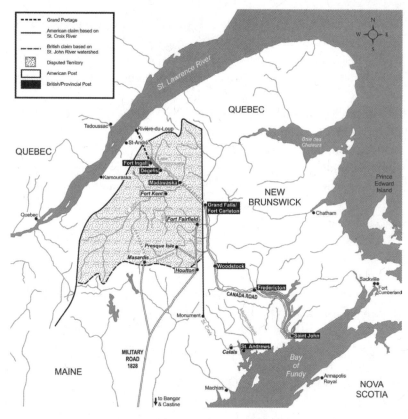

Military posts during the garrison period. 175

Chapter Five

The Disputed Territory Partitioned

*[O]ur true policy was to proceed silently and, quietly
strengthening ourselves on the Territory, and while the two
Governments were negotiating we should decide the question*
— Charles Jarvis to Governor John Fairfield,
January 7, 1840

The Aroostook War focused the attention of the United States and Britain
on the need to eliminate lingering sources of tension in their relations.
The unresolved boundary was not the only issue adversely affecting
Anglo-American relations. Rebel Canadians who had fled to the northern
states continued their cross-border raids with the assistance of American
sympathizers; other crises erupted to further deteriorate relations. Taken
collectively, these posed a serious risk of war. Meanwhile, the boundary
negotiations continued their desultory pace, and friction between the
Maine land agent's men and British authorities kept tensions high in
the Madawaska settlement.

Troop withdrawals began following the signing of the March 25, 1839,
agreement, but not all could be dismissed immediately, as they still had
tasks to complete. The embodied New Brunswick militia were to receive
pay and rations until April 10 to give them sufficient time to demobilize.
A detachment of thirty-four militiamen, which included four axemen,
was retained at Woodstock. Another group of twenty-four militiamen,
also including four axemen, was kept at Tobique and the Mouth of the
Aroostook, presumably to guard the timber boom. Yet another detachment of twenty-five militiamen remained at St. Andrews, to guard Her
Majesty's stores there. These troops appear to have remained in service

until sometime in June. The York Light Dragoons were kept in service until April 30, probably employed as couriers. The headquarters of the 69th Regiment of Foot was established at Woodstock while that of the 36th Regiment returned to Fredericton. Garrisons were retained at Woodstock, Tobique, and the Mouth of the Aroostook and Grand Falls. Meanwhile, the 11th Regiment and the Royal Artillery detachment left the Madawaska settlement and returned to Lower Canada.

Similar activities occurred on the other side of the Commissioners' Line. Friction continued between the land agent's posse and the Maine militia. On March 22, Jarvis asked Hodsdon to detail thirty or forty men to accompany Thomas Bartlett to look for trespassers who were known to be on the River de Chute. The militiamen balked, however, complaining that the posse received a higher rate of pay. Seeing this discontent, Bartlett returned to Fort Fairfield and set out again with a detachment of the posse. Hodsdon immediately detailed another group of militia to follow after Bartlett, and it performed satisfactorily. As this was unfolding, Hodsdon was told to withdraw his troops in accordance with the agreement. On April 1, he issued his orders and the next day the Maine militia began returning to their homes. A detachment from Bachelder's force remained at Masardis to guard public stores. Two companies from Hodsdon's force under Major James Smith stayed at Fort Fairfield and Presque Isle of the Aroostook to protect the boom and guard stores until the Land Agent had assembled a force to take over these duties. It appears that the land agent's force made the transition from posse to a Corps of Volunteers during this period.

While the withdrawal of troops on the New Brunswick side proceeded smoothly, another conflict between the Maine land agent and the state militia developed on or about March 30. Jarvis had sent Assistant Provisional Land Agent Alvin Nye, with a mixture of posse and militiamen from Bachelder's force, to the Fish River, where they were to build a boom to prevent any timber cut during the winter from being floated out to market in Saint John. Jarvis and McIntire were fully aware that this move to the Fish River violated the intent, if not the words, of the March 25 agreement. When Hodsdon learned about this, he ordered the militiamen to return. Jarvis asked if some, perhaps a hundred, could enlist as volunteers with the land agent. As he had no orders relating to this, Hodsdon said that they could not, which forced Jarvis to end his first expedition to Fish River.

Jarvis and McIntire were not discouraged, however, as they also had Governor Fairfield's support for asserting Maine's jurisdiction over the Fish. Moreover, the resolve of February 20 had authorized "that a sufficient military force be forthwith stationed on the Aroostook River, west of the boundary-line of the State, as established by the Treaty of 1783; and on the river St. John, if found practicable." Having gained control of the Aroostook Valley, it was now time to move north to the St. John River. As a result, in the aftermath of the Aroostook War, events along the Aroostook and Fish rivers developed along different paths.

Tensions still ran high along the Aroostook River. Despite the agreement that Scott had brokered, Jarvis expected an attack on the boom at Fort Fairfield by lumbermen wanting to float their timber to market without having to pay the Maine land agent. To guard against this, Jarvis proposed building a blockhouse on the hill overlooking the river, another alongside the river close to the boom, and a third on the far (north) side of the river. Once again, friction developed between the land agent and the militia: Jarvis thought the militia should build the blockhouses, but the militia did not see it as their task, forcing Jarvis to employ his small force of volunteers. On April 9, Assistant Land Agent [Captain] William Parrott took charge of the volunteers and put his men to work building a blockhouse by the boom. On the same day, Captain Bartlett set out with ten volunteers to look for trespassers along River de Chute. Jarvis had asked for twenty militiamen to accompany him, but Smith had declined, saying his orders did not allow him to do so. Besides arresting trespassers, Bartlett was also to burn their camps and obstruct the river so logs could not be run down it. The next day, he encountered and arrested eight lumbermen and seized their teams. One of the prisoners, said to have been a boy, escaped. Fearing that a rescue party would come to their aide, Bartlett began preparations to return to Fort Fairfield on the eleventh. His fears were justified, as a group of twenty-eight men with muskets and fowling pieces appeared to free the prisoners. The leader of the rescue party was John Vanning, a lumberman and New Brunswick militia officer. As the volunteers were outnumbered and outgunned, having only horse pistols for weapons, Bartlett decided not to make a fight of it. Vanning told the captured lumbermen that they were free to leave, but Bartlett held a trump card and played it. He told Asa Harvey and John Karney, the owners of the teams, that if they returned with him to Fort Fairfield they might be able to convince the land agent not to destroy their timber, but if they left with Vanning, Bartlett would return and destroy all the timber. Because taking Bartlett's offer was the only way they might salvage their winter's work, they agreed to go with him to plead their case with the land agent. Jarvis blamed this fiasco on the failure of the Maine militia to support him. He also thought that the success of the "mob," as he referred to it, in almost releasing the prisoners would embolden them and thus increase the risk to the boom at Fort Fairfield.

On April 12, the irons used to link the logs in the boom arrived and the boom was completed — just in time, as the river ice was beginning to break up. While parties of volunteers looked for trespassers, especially along River de Chute, the main effort continued at the boom and on the blockhouses. Men from New Brunswick were frequently in the area, and several were suspected of involvement in the capture of McIntire and his party; they thus represented a possible threat. Timber nevertheless began arriving at the boom.

The immediate problem was to separate "permitted" timber cut under licences issued by Massachusetts from trespass timber, a difficult task; there was also the risk that some illegal timber would pass through the boom. Assistant Land Agent Captain William Parrott's answer was to stop the passage of all timber until McIntire could give him more specific instructions — even Colonel Webster and Shepard Cary, both of whom had supported the land agent during the Aroostook War, found their timber held up. The presence of the land agent's volunteers was proving a double-edged sword for the lumbermen.

Fearing that Webster, Cary, and other lumbermen would take action to break the boom, in early May Parrott issued orders that proscribed the area around the boom and authorized the use of force to prevent any attempt to remove it. To add to his difficulties, on May 5, a "molasses mutiny" broke out among a group of nine volunteers who complained they were not receiving their molasses ration. As their insubordination threatened to spread through the volunteers, Parrott took firm action, quickly dismissing them and having them escorted from Fort Fairfield as far as Houlton, from where they were to find their own way home. He also wrote to McIntire requesting that the molasses ration be sent up immediately. Meanwhile, McIntire's instructions arrived, and by May 6 the work of passing timber through the boom was under way, and was expected to be completed by May 19. Of course, this timber still had to pass the New Brunswick boom at the mouth of the Aroostook River, where it would be subject to a fine of 8 shillings per ton. For most of the month, the provincial boom was under the charge of a seizing officer, H.M. Garden, who had a guard of one officer and twenty men of the 69th Regiment plus a detachment of militia from the 2nd Battalion, Carleton County Militia.

By early July, the major construction work at Fort Fairfield had been completed. Lieutenant Philip J. Bainbrigge of the Royal Engineers visited the fort and sketched a map of it. The lower blockhouse overlooked the boom across the Aroostook River and mounted a small iron cannon to cover it. The upper blockhouse, on Fort Hill, was surrounded by a palisade and mounted a brass 24-pounder howitzer and a brass 12-pounder cannon. The two blockhouses were about two hundred metres apart. Four log barracks were located along the road to the north of the upper blockhouse. The position was thus snug and secure and well prepared to defend the boom from any attacker.

By mid-July, Parrott had begun to auction off the seized trespass timber at the Fort Fairfield boom. The price of timber at Saint John was said to be running very high, so it was thought that the timber at the boom might fetch as much as $4.22 per ton, but in the event it sold for only the minimum bid of $3.00 per ton. Indeed, the economics of the timber trade remain a bit of a mystery. In 1839, about 60,000 tons was exported through the port of Saint John, mostly to Britain. In November, Parrott reported that, according to a British newspaper, white pine was selling for approximately £4 5s 10d, or $20.90, per ton. The cost of duties and fines—about $5.00—before the timber reached the St. John River, and of floating it to Saint John, resquaring it, and shipping it to England, could

The Upper Blockhouse, one of two built at Fort Fairfield in
1839 by the Maine land agent's volunteers; attacked by
New Brunswick lumbermen on September 8, 1839.
Courtesy of the Fort Fairfield Sesquicentennial Committee

not have allowed much room for profit. Yet it was a large-scale business,
and profits evidently were sufficient to justify the effort.

As fall approached, Parrott became aware that many lumbermen were
preparing to enter the Aroostook Valley to cut timber under the pretext
of possessing permits from Massachusetts. Parrott decided not to allow
anyone with teams, provisions, or anything else connected with lumbering
operations to pass by Fort Fairfield, an action that Jarvis and McIntire
endorsed. Notice of this policy was posted around September 5, but the
step proved too much for the New Brunswick lumbermen to endure, and
so they decided to take action. On the evening of September 7, a group
of them gathered once again at Tibbits's store in Tobique. The store had
been used by the commissariat during the Aroostook War, and some forty
to sixty men took some of the militia arms that had been left there for
safekeeping and set out to attack Fort Fairfield. As they approached the

Reconstruction of the Lower Blockhouse, Fort Fairfield,
built close to the log boom to protect it. Photograph by the author

fort at about 2 o'clock the next morning, an alert sentry spotted them and
fired. The attackers "took to their heels" and quickly returned to Tobique,
in their haste leaving behind "[t]wo muskets and five bayonets, three hats,
an axe, some shoes and even boots." The arms were replaced in the store
and the lumbermen dispersed.

The attack, however paltry, shocked the leaders of New Brunswick.
It was not the behaviour expected of a British subject; worse, a militia
officer was thought to have been the leader. The raid constituted a major
breech in civil order, the very kind of vigilante action Lieutenant-Governor
Harvey had crushed the previous winter. MacLauchlan, still warden of
the Disputed Territory, had been at Grand Falls, where he had been assisting George William Featherstonhaugh, who with Lieutenant-Colonel
Richard Z. Mudge, Royal Engineers, was about to begin a British survey
to locate the elusive "highlands." Upon hearing the news, MacLauchlan

and Featherstonhaugh set out for Fort Fairfield; there, they met separately with Captain Parrott. The assistant land agent was not overly upset by the raid, which he described as an "affair too *ridiculous* to be taken seriously." He had a list of eighteen men who he thought had been involved, and he suspected Tibbits of having aided the attackers.

MacLauchlan, who no doubt reflected the sentiments of many in New Brunswick when he referred to it as a "most disgraceful affair," then began a formal investigation of behalf of Harvey. MacLauchlan concluded that the raid had been planned in Woodstock, that some known lumbermen, such as John Vanning and Punderson Beardsley, had been involved, and that they had been aided by merchants and lumbermen from the Tobique area. Tibbits, questioned about his role, claimed that, although he knew men had gathered near his house that evening, he had no knowledge of the raid. MacLauchlan arranged for the muskets in Tibbits's store to be removed to the garrison at Grand Falls. The only man punished for participating in the raid was Waterloo veteran Captain William McKenzie, singled out because he was a militia officer, though only one of at least four involved.

McKenzie's situation provides interesting insight into the attitudes of the time. A corporal in the 52nd Regiment of Foot at the Battle of Waterloo, where he was wounded, he moved to New Brunswick after his release from the army, married, and founded the settlement of McKenzie Corners, located between Woodstock and Houlton. On September 7, he had been recruited "at a late hour," those calling on him using a copy of a speech by the Duke of Wellington decrying Maine's actions in seizing the Aroostook Valley to induce McKenzie to join them. This appeal to his patriotism and his respect for the duke were sufficient incentives. Once he realized what was being planned, he could not quit for fear of being thought a coward. Despite his punishment and humiliation, he did not name the men who had recruited him. Harvey reprimanded McKenzie in Militia Orders and revoked his commission because he was "the lead in this unwarranted and absurd attempt." From the start, however, McKenzie—who acknowledged his mistake and vowed not to repeat it—had supporters such as Lieutenant-Colonel Maxwell, who urged leniency. A year later, in September 1840, Harvey received a petition from forty-four prominent citizens of the

The Waterloo medal, issued to everyone who participated in the Battle of Waterloo on June 18, 1815, or its related battles, including Captain William McKenzie, who was wounded in the foot; his devotion to the Duke of Wellington, forged no doubt in the battle, later contributed to his disgrace. Courtesy of Andrew John Monkhouse

Woodstock area asking that McKenzie's commission be restored. Harvey endorsed the petition and forwarded it to London with the comment that the US government had pardoned "[m]any of the individuals engaged in the recent invasions of the Canadas." Lord John Russell, the secretary of state for the Colonies, agreed and McKenzie got his commission back. The raid of September 7 was the last event in what became known as the Lumbermen's Resistance.

As the fall of 1839 progressed, settlers on both sides of the Commissioners' Line along the Aroostook River gradually adapted to the new regime. Parrott confiscated boats and supplies being taken up river, including those owned by fellow Americans Colonel Webster and Captain Pilsbury, who, with their partner, James Taylor of Fredericton, seem to have settled their differences with Parrott in court. On November 11, one of the Fort Fairfield blockhouses caught fire and suffered minor damage, perhaps sparking a story that lumbermen had burned it down. Then, late in 1839 or early in 1840, the boom at the Mouth of the Aroostook—in which both Punderson Beardsley and James Taylor held interests — was returned to its civilian owners. In 1843, as a final irony, the Aroostook boom having washed out, the Fort Fairfield boom was sold to a group of American and British lumbermen, including Shepard Cary, who moved it to the Mouth of the Aroostook, but on the New Brunswick side of the Line.

Although the March 25, 1839 agreement had clarified the lines of jurisdiction along the Aroostook, things were not so clear farther north. Since receiving Buckmore's report, Maine had been concerned about the amount of illegally cut trespass timber on the Fish River. In February, the Maine posse had made a pass through the area and driven off or captured a number of lumbermen. In late March, a second expedition was recalled due to a jurisdictional squabble between the land agent and the Maine militia. Now that Maine controlled the Aroostook Valley, the land agent again turned his attention to the Fish River and the illegal cutting occurring there.

Before Nye left on his abortive mission to Fish River at the end of March, Jarvis had given him explicit orders that he was to prevent the passage of timber down the Fish River by building a boom with a blockhouse to protect it. If threatened by a British force, he was to defend the honour of Maine. This meant that he was to defend himself if practicable but withdraw or surrender if facing a superior force. Under no circumstances was he to cross the St. John River to the north side and violate the jurisdictional limits of New Brunswick — clear *de facto* recognition of British control over the northern part of the Disputed Territory. It is equally clear, however, that Maine considered the right, or southern, bank of the St. John in this area to be in its area of jurisdiction. This contradicted the British position that the Madawaska settlement extended along both banks of the St. John to the Fish and beyond. Since Nye's mission could have been seen as a violation of the recent tripartite agreement, this was an interesting direction to receive. In early April, Nye set out a second time for the Fish River, reaching Soldier Pond, where he set to work building a boom and blockhouse. Supplies were a problem, so the post was to grow some of its own food, and Nye had been instructed to seek out John Baker to learn the lay of the land and to obtain potatoes and turnips to use for seed.

Finding his presence unchallenged by the British, Nye moved down to the mouth of the Fish to an island, where he built a new boom joining it to the south shore. This enabled him to control any timber coming down the Fish and in the channel between the island and the south shore. He also built a blockhouse for protection and named his post Fort Jarvis. The presence of Nye and his party was soon noticed, however, and on April 13 Thomas Sutton reported their arrival to Captain Coote, commanding a company of the 69th Regiment at Grand Falls. Sutton had spoken with Baker, who said that the Americans were going to stay "for as long as they found it necessary to prevent the timber from being taken away." This disturbing news was quickly forwarded to Fredericton.

There, Harvey, upset that the American presence on the Fish had gone unreported for some period of time, reprimanded MacLauchlan for his apparent lack of attention to the Disputed Territory. MacLauchlan had also been supervising the improvement of the road to the Canadas; Harvey now suggested that he concentrate on his main task—that of preventing the cutting of trespass timber—and delegate his road-building responsibilities to a deputy. Offended by these instructions, MacLauchlan submitted his resignation but it was rejected, Harvey instead advising him to stay in his post until relieved. The episode appears to have been the start of an unfortunate rift that would later contribute to Harvey's dismissal from office. The two men had served along the Niagara frontier during the War of 1812—Harvey as a lieutenant colonel on the staff in the position of deputy adjutant general and MacLauchlan as a lieutenant in the Light Company of the 104th (New Brunswick) Regiment of Foot—but despite this shared experience, disagreement about the Disputed Territory forced them apart.

Once in position, Nye began to stop the passage of timber down the Fish River and even some down the St. John. He also challenged MacLauchlan's authority as warden of the Disputed Territory. On May 10, having learned that MacLauchlan was preparing to drive seized trespass timber located on the St. John above the Fish, Nye wrote to tell him that the timber was under the jurisdiction of Maine and that he would not permit MacLauchlan to remove it. MacLauchlan forwarded the letter to

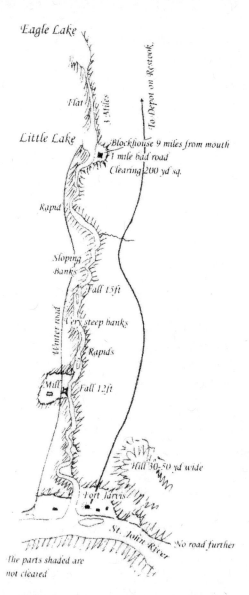

Eagle Lake

Flat

3 Miles

To Depot on Restook

Little Lake

Blockhouse 9 miles from mouth
1 mile bad road
Clearing 200 yd sq.

Rapid

Sloping
Banks

Fall 15ft

Winter road

Very steep banks

Rapids

Mill

Fall 12ft

Hill 30-50 yd wide

Fort Jarvis

St. John River

No road further

The parts shaded are
not cleared

Fort Kent, initially Fort Jarvis, established by the Maine land agent's
volunteers in early 1839. Original sketch by Lieutenant Philip John
Bainbrigge, Royal Engineers, adapted by Béatrice Craig. Courtesy of Béatrice Craig

The original blockhouse, Fort Kent, built by the Maine land agent's volunteers in 1839. Photo by Howard W. Marshall from the Maine Acadian Cultural Survey Collection; with permission of the American Folklife Center, Library of Congress, Washington, DC

Fredericton; while he waited for direction, Nye acted. That same day, the British deputy surveyor, William J. Burton, passed Nye proceeding up the St. John with a group of about thirty men, eighteen of whom were armed with muskets and fixed bayonets; not surprisingly, John Baker was with them. Upriver, Nye's men encountered a party of twenty led by Elias Yerxa, whom MacLauchlan had hired to drive trespass timber down from the St. Francis River. Nye and twelve armed men entered the drivers' camp, escorted them at bayonet point to their canoes, and ordered them to leave the area immediately. A few days later, certainly before May 15, Nye reported that he "had driven off a gang of trespassers with Mr. McLaughlin [*sic*] at their head who with threats set off down river to procure reinforcements." Nye sent Baker to Fort Fairfield to obtain reinforcements, and Parrott immediately sent twenty-five men led by Captain Bartlett to his aid. It is not clear if this incident was separate from that of May 10, but tensions clearly were once again beginning to mount along the Upper St. John River.

At this point, Harvey missed an opportunity to assert British control over the Fish River. He had considered ordering the company of the 69th Regiment at Grand Falls to expel the volunteers, but instead chose the diplomatic approach. On May 14, he sent a letter to General Scott stating that, since the Fish River was within the "Upper Settlement of Madawaska," the volunteers' presence violated the terms of the agreement he and Scott and Fairfield had signed. Harvey also stated that MacLauchlan had been directed to remain within "the [Madawaska] settlement rather than risk collision." Nothing came of this letter of protest—Scott was now far away and without influence over Maine's actions.

Events continued to unfold. On June 6, Thomas Baillie, the commissioner of Crown Lands for New Brunswick, and Rufus McIntire, the Maine land agent, met at Bangor. Baillie laid out his complaints. The first issue was the definition of the Madawaska settlement, which the British claimed included both sides of the St. John River, while Maine considered it referred only to settlement on the north bank. McIntire conceded that Nye had exceeded his instructions, but Nye would remain at the Fish River as, according to Maine, it was not part of the Madawaska settlement and therefore his presence did not violate the agreement. Baillie protested, but to no avail: Maine was now firmly positioned on the St. John, west of the Commissioners' Line.

Maine's real intentions were revealed in a letter from Jarvis to Fairfield dated January 7, 1840. In it Jarvis said, "[o]ur true policy is to proceed silently and quietly, strengthening ourselves on the Territory, and while the two countries were negotiating, we should decide the question." In truth, this is exactly what the British had done in the northern portion of the Disputed Territory. Negotiate or not, Maine now controlled the southern portion, and the Disputed Territory effectively had been partitioned west of the Commissioners' Line, along the line of the St. John River. The only area left in doubt was that part of the Madawaska settlement that lay on the south bank of the St. John. Maine's presence on the St. John now represented a tangible threat to the communications route at the crucial junction of the St. John and the Madawaska and to the British inhabitants in the Madawaska settlement.

These events led to the gradual militarization of the Disputed Territory. By 1839, Maine had established two strongholds within the southern half, at Fort Fairfield and Fort Jarvis (later Fort Kent). The British, too, were making contingency plans as the Aroostook War crisis wound down. The rebellions in the Canadas had reinforced the strategic importance of the Grand Communications Route through New Brunswick, and Maine had shown the route's vulnerability to hostile actions. In mid-March 1839, Sir John Colborne indicated in a letter to Harvey that he believed the boundary question would again be submitted to arbitration. In the interim, he also believed that it was our "duty to do everything in our power to diminish the chances of hostilities by our forbearance but [at the same time] to make active preparations for war. The Commissariat Department has sent supplies to Rivière-du-Loup for the Madawaska Settlement Detachment for three months. I have ordered boats to be built on the Lake Temiscouata and shall endeavour to improve the road from the valley of the St. Lawrence to the Lake and to assist you in completing the route to Madawaska." Harvey agreed, stating, "we must exert ourselves in the improvement of our communication between the Madawaska and the St. Lawrence," and by late March he had ordered MacLauchlan to work on this.

One of their first steps was to rebuild Fort Carleton in Grand Falls. Major F.W. Whingates, Royal Engineers, was assigned the task. By April 5, he was able to report that three barracks capable of accommodating 210 men along with a cookhouse and a privy had been built with the assistance of Sir John Caldwell's men. The fort still lacked a storehouse, guardroom, and a surrounding palisade. On July 25, Harvey could report that he and Colborne were improving the route and establishing a series of posts along it to facilitate the movement of troops. The rebuilding of Fort Carleton marks the start of the consolidation or garrison period of this story.

British plans also included improving the outpost at Dégelis (Quebec), where barracks for the officers and soldiers, along with a cookhouse and guardroom, had been built on the right bank of the Madawaska River about two miles below the outlet of Lake Temiscouata. In June 1839,

Colborne established a small garrison of thirteen soldiers at Fort Ingall (Cabano, Quebec), named for Lieutenant Frederick Lennox Ingall of the 15th Regiment of Foot, who had first surveyed the site to determine its suitability for a military post. By the summer, barracks for soldiers and officers had been built. These sites would be developed further as border tensions continued. Plans were also made to build a permanent post at Woodstock, "to protect the line of communications between that Province [New Brunswick] and Canada" but this was not done. The finishing touch was the construction of a blockhouse at the mouth of the Madawaska River in fall 1841; a replica now stands on the site.

The British increased their presence in the Disputed Territory in fall 1839 by reinforcing the garrison at Fort Ingall with two companies of the 11th Regiment under Brevet Major William Chambre — a precautionary measure following the raid on Fort Fairfield in September. The first company arrived in November, the second the next month. Lieutenant Philip J. Bainbrigge, Royal Engineers, was sent in November to "place the Barracks at Temiscouata in a state of defence." He also reconnoitered the country, which included a daring reconnaissance to Fort Jarvis, where a new blockhouse was being built to replace the original structure, and up the Fish River to Soldier Pond, where the blockhouse had been recently abandoned.

More excitement took place the following year, when Colonel Gorham Parks, a former congressman from Maine and a United States marshal, arrived in the Madawaska settlement in August to conduct the sixth US census. Harvey sent MacLauchlan to protest the census but, as it was a federal and not a Maine undertaking, he did not stop Gorham Parks's work.

The US presidential elections sparked the next significant crisis. On November 2, a meeting was held at the Fort Jarvis blockhouse to vote for the president and vice-president. According to Francis Rice, who attended in his capacity as a British official, about a hundred persons were present, "principally Americans... [and] ... a few French Canadians of the lower class." When Rice protested the legality of the meeting, Assistant Land Agent Stover Rines, who had replaced Nye the previous summer, threatened to arrest him. Rice was removed from the meeting and roughly

As tensions rose in the Disputed Territory, the British built a blockhouse at Petit Sault (Edmundston) in 1841 to protect the Grand Communications Route and to counter the influence of the Maine land agent's volunteers at nearby Fort Kent. LAC, C-40144

used by John Baker and some other Americans. Rines, however, prevented further harm from coming to him, but also stated that he would arrest any British officials who tried to exercise jurisdiction along the St. John River north of the Madawaska.

This latest insult to a British official, and an American claim to jurisdiction above the Madawaska, pushed Harvey's patience to the breaking point. On November 13, he asked Lord Sydenham, the governor general of British North America, if the British were simply going to protest Maine's actions or would they take stronger steps by moving in a military force "to give confidence and protection to the Queen's subjects, and support to the civil authorities." The next day, Harvey sent another letter expressing his concern about Maine's attempts to take control of a third of the population of the Madawaska settlement and blocking the line of communication. He proposed building blockhouses opposite the Fish River and at the junction

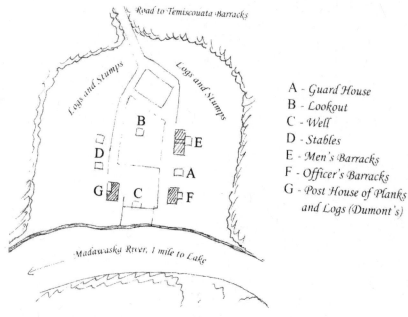

A - *Guard House*
B - *Lookout*
C - *Well*
D - *Stables*
E - *Men's Barracks*
F - *Officer's Barracks*
G - *Post House of Planks and Logs (Dumont's)*

The post at Dégelis (Quebec), built in 1839 to provide shelter for troops on the march and to guard the entrance to Lake Temiscouata.

Original sketch by Lieutenant Philip John Bainbrigge, Royal Engineers, adapted by Béatrice Craig.

Courtesy of Béatrice Craig

of the Madawaska and St. John rivers. He also suggested garrisoning them with an armed posse or police force, as Maine had done. A non-military force, moreover, would give Maine no cause for complaint. Three days later, Harvey wrote again, saying he had decided against sending troops but instead wanted a civil party or posse under the direction of the warden and local magistrates, MacLauchlan having assured him an armed posse was possible. He had also sent MacLauchlan to argue the case with Lord Sydenham himself, instructing him to answer any questions frankly. MacLauchlan did so, responding to the governor general's query that he actually preferred a military force, which led to his cross-examination upon his return to Fredericton.

Harvey was further embarrassed when his advisors opined that it was not legal to form an American-style armed posse. By this time, Harvey's dithering about a posse was testing Lord Sydenham's patience, and the governor general took advantage of MacLauchlan's presence in Montreal to direct him to communicate directly with his secretary, to keep him up to date on events in the Disputed Territory, rather than have to rely on second-hand news from Harvey.

The British authorities were not pleased with Harvey's handling of the American presence on the Fish River. In May 1839, Harvey had considered sending a company of infantry to the Madawaska settlement to assert British authority, to provide support for the settlers, and to prevent any interference with the mail courier, but he was deterred by the reassuring responses he had received from the American authorities. It was here that Harvey's trust and friendship with Winfield Scott let him down, but there was little that Scott and international diplomacy could do in the face of Maine's aggressive stance. Force had to be met with force, and Harvey had not done so. This inactivity had allowed Maine volunteers to establish themselves firmly at Fort Jarvis. Then, after Colborne reinforced the garrison at Fort Ingall in December 1839, Fairfield had sent Harvey a letter about this movement that was "so clearly in violation of the ar-rangement" that General Scott had negotiated. Harvey's reply had an apologetic tone in which he stated that the movement of troops had "been made by authority superior to mine." Harvey's superiors did not appreciate this revelation of division within the British position. They also did not like his habit of corresponding directly with Fairfield instead of through the proper diplomatic channels in Washington. As a consequence, Harvey was directed not to take an active role in the boundary discussions.

Sydenham also informed Harvey that troops were being sent to protect British interests in the area in accordance with London's direction that he was "not to permit Maine to occupy or possess land to the north of the St. John's" and to "maintain in perfect security the communications by the Madawaska between Fredericton and Quebec." In December 1840, two companies of the 56th Regiment arrived at Madawaska to reinforce the company of the 56th already at Fort Ingall and the small detachment that had been placed at Dégelis in June. Fairfield, of course, protested this to Harvey, and President

Van Buren requested "measures to ensure the immediate withdrawal of these troops from our territory, or to expel them," but without success.

Harvey's handling of the post-Aroostook War period led to his dismissal from office and, in April 1841, to the arrival of his successor, Sir William Colebrooke. Meanwhile, through 1840 and 1841, the presence of Maine volunteers in the Madawaska settlement continued to generate friction. Maine seemed to be making the St. John River the line of partition, which concerned the British by challenging their *de facto* jurisdiction over the part of the Madawaska settlement that lay on the right, or southern, bank of the river. It also meant that British-Acadian citizens could find themselves becoming Americans. The Acadians, too, opposed this change and informed Colebrooke of their desire to remain British.

The British were hesitant to station troops on the south bank of the St. John, as the US government would see this as a violation of the agreement. Yet the presence of Americans in the region had an impact on the life of the community. In April 1841, John Baker was arrested and convicted of aiding the desertion of seven soldiers of the 56th Regiment from the Madawaska garrison. Captain Rines, the commander of the posse at the Fish River, was implicated as well. Because of the real possibility of collision between the agents of Maine and New Brunswick, MacLauchlan was directed to "enjoin the strictest caution ... with regard to his conduct and ... abstain from interference with the American civil posse." Meanwhile, the US government, at the insistence of Maine, which was finding the civil posse expensive to maintain, considered stationing federal troops at Forts Fairfield and Jarvis. The British were not initially in favour of this step, as it would promote a sense of permanence to the American presence along the St. John, but, because of the ongoing problems with the conduct of the volunteers, accepted it as "a measure of wise precaution and probably the only one that would effectively guard against collision."

In early September 1841, one company of the First Artillery Regiment, US Army, stationed at Hancock Barracks in Houlton, was sent to garrison Fort Fairfield and the former Fort Jarvis, recently renamed Fort Kent in honour of Maine's new governor, Edward Kent. Because this happened before a formal agreement had been made with the British, Sydenham

Fort Ingall, by Lieutenant Philip John Bainbrigge, Royal Engineers, circa 1840; the fort was constructed in 1839 and 1840 to serve as a post along the Grand Communications Route and to guard the southern entrance of the Grand Portage. LAC C-017787

took the opportunity to order part of the garrison at Madawaska to move to the south bank, "with a view to more effectually protect Her Majesty's subjects, and to mark, most distinctly, our determination to maintain our jurisdiction there." The British reinforced this move by finally building a blockhouse at the junction of the Madawaska and St. John rivers.

By 1841, the Disputed Territory in effect had been partitioned and garrisoned. British regulars were located in a series of garrisons along the course of the Grand Communications Route, while the US Army had taken over Forts Fairfield and Kent from the civilian volunteers of the Maine land agent. The only deployment that proved—ultimately—to be misplaced was the British force guarding the Madawaska settlement on the southern bank of the St. John River. Despite claims by both governments that the presence of regular British and US troops did not give an air of permanency to this arrangement, it should have been quite clear that it did.

The garrison period was now fully developed, the border anything but undefended. How long could the standoff continue? Moreover, the Maine-New Brunswick border dispute was not the only source of friction between the United States and Britain. The Aroostook War had almost sparked a third Anglo-American war, now other incidents threatened to do so.

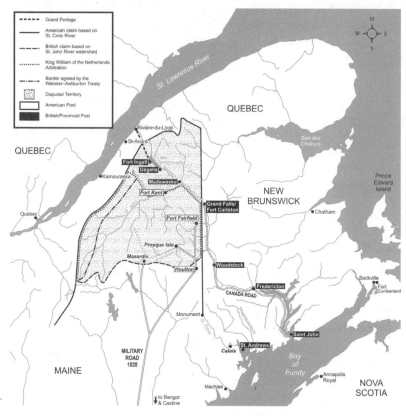

The Ashburton-Webster Treaty finally determined
the boundary line through the Disputed Territory. MB

Chapter Six

The Ashburton-Webster Treaty

Blessed are the peacemakers
— President John Tyler, June 23, 1842,
celebrating the successful completion of the
Ashburton-Webster negotiations

The late 1830s and the early 1840s were a tumultuous time in Anglo-American relations. While there had been a long-standing uneasiness in the interactions between the two nations, recent events had caused tensions to escalate to the brink of war on at least two occasions. The rebellions in Upper and Lower Canada in 1837 and 1838 generated considerable American sympathy. Many of the rebels had fled to the northern states and, aided by their American allies, conducted raids into the Canadas, keeping the border in a state of alert. When the Aroostook War crisis erupted, war again appeared likely. It would not take much more, both the US and British governments feared, to ignite another Anglo-American war. But the next crisis that threatened war, the *Caroline* affair, actually hastened the negotiations that ultimately settled the eastern border between the United States of America and what became the Dominion of Canada in 1867.

The *Caroline* affair became a long running source of friction between the United States and Britain. It started in late 1837 when a group of rebels from Upper Canada fled to New York state, established a base on Navy Island in the Niagara River, and hired an American vessel, the *Caroline,* as a supply ship. On December 29, a military force from Upper Canada captured the *Caroline* and burnt her. During the affair an American citizen, Amos Durfee, was killed. This violation of US territory and the murder of one of its citizens outraged the American public. In time, the crisis subsided but in September 1840 it rose again to prominence when Alexander McLeod was arrested in Lewiston, New York, accused of being part of the raiding party that had captured the *Caroline*. More important, he had been bragging that he had killed Durfee, and was now charged with his murder. When his case went to trial in 1841, he became a lightning rod for anti-British sentiment in the United States. During the trial, it became apparent that McLeod might be executed if found guilty. The British protested to the US government that the trial was illegal under international law, but Washington could not intervene in a trial held under the jurisdiction of the state of New York. As the trial progressed, international relations deteriorated. The British government told Fox, the British ambassador in Washington, to leave the United States if McLeod was convicted. Lord Sydenham, as governor general of British North America and commander of the British forces there, received a warning order to prepare for war. Ships of the Royal Navy were gathered and readied for action. Fortunately, on October 12, 1841, the jury found McLeod not guilty, and the crisis receded.

A month later, the issue of slavery and British efforts to suppress the slave trade became another source of friction. This time it was the southern states that were enraged by Britain's actions. In November 1841, the crisis flared when the slaves aboard the American ship *Creole* mutinied, took over the vessel, and sailed it to a British port in the Bahamas. In accordance with the British Emancipation Act of 1833, most of the slaves were set free; a number were kept in custody, charged in the death of a crew member. British refusal to extradite these prisoners to the United States stirred up emotions, especially in the southern slave-owning states, and created strong anti-British feelings in an area not normally anglophobic.

By now, both the United States and Britain realized that it was time to resolve the issues that were creating the ongoing friction and ill-will between the two nations. Fortunately, recent changes of government in

Facing page: Alexander Baring (Lord Ashburton), the distinguished British banker chosen to negotiate a treaty with his US counterpart, Daniel Webster. Library of Congress

both countries had brought in administrations more amenable to resolving their differences. In the 1840 presidential elections, Martin Van Buren and the Democrats lost to the Whigs under William Henry Harrison. In early 1841, the new administration was sworn in and Daniel Webster, an anglophile and well thought of by the British, became secretary of state. Harrison, though, suddenly died a month after taking office and was succeeded by his vice-president, John Tyler.

In London, Sir Robert Peel replaced William Lamb, 2nd Viscount Melbourne, as prime minister, while Lord Aberdeen became the new foreign secretary. Both men were known for their conciliatory approach to domestic and foreign problems. In late 1841, the British announced the appointment of Alexander Baring, Lord Ashburton, as special minister to Washington with a brief to resolve the outstanding issues with the United States. Baring was an excellent choice, having retired from the British banking firm of Baring Brothers and Company, which had long-standing ties with the United States. In the 1790s, Baring had visited the United States, purchased a large tract of land in northern Massachusetts (eastern Maine) from William Bingham, and married one of his daughters. He had no financial interest in any part of the Disputed Territory, but he did have an interest in the area and its people. While in the Americas, Baring had travelled from Quebec to New Brunswick over the Grand Communications Route and so was familiar with the area in question. Later, Baring Brothers had helped to finance the 1803 Louisiana Purchase by the United States. Coincidentally, Daniel Webster had acted for years as Baring Brothers's legal consul in the United States. One could hardly have asked for a better pair of men to work together.

On April 4, 1842, Ashburton arrived in the United States and negotiations soon began. With regard to the Disputed Territory, Ashburton was instructed not to accept anything less than the 1831 arbitration award, which would secure the Grand Communications Route for Britain. The Duke of Wellington also wanted the border pushed back from the height of land overlooking the St. Lawrence River, which would prevent the Americans from threatening British ships on the river in the event of a war. If possible, the Madawaska settlement was to be kept intact.

Daniel Webster, US secretary of state. Library of Congress

Meanwhile, Webster had been busy preparing the ground even before the negotiations were announced. In mid-1841, he had begun a public information campaign in the Maine newspapers. This had been suggested to him by Francis O.J. Smith, a Maine politician, attorney, and newspaper publisher. Using Secret Service funds authorized by the president, Smith began a series of newspaper articles designed to sway public opinion in Maine toward accepting a compromise boundary settlement. Webster had another trick up his sleeve. Jared Sparks had found maps in the Paris archives that related to the 1783 Treaty of Paris negotiations. According to red lines on the maps attributed to Benjamin Franklin and Baron von Steuben, the British claim included the entire watershed of the St. John River, a much larger area than the Disputed Territory. Webster made these maps known to Maine politicians, leading them to believe it was evidence that weakened the US claim to the Disputed Territory and the border sketched out in the 1783 Treaty of Paris. This became known as the "battle of the maps." Webster also learned that Maine's Whigs and Democrats were prepared to accept a compromise boundary but, for political reasons, could not be seen to be in favour of it. In exchange for giving up land, they wanted free navigation on the St. John River—then essential for the economic development of the Disputed Territory—and reimbursement from the federal government for past costs of defending the territory. Of course, this information was not shared with Ashburton.

Having softened up the opposition in Maine, Webster was now ready for negotiations, which he took the unprecedented step of inviting commissioners from Maine and Massachusetts to observe. Webster felt this would speed up the process. Governor Fairfield of Maine sent four ardent supporters of his state's claims: Judge William Pitt Preble, who had vigorously opposed the 1831 arbitration, former governor Edward Kent, Edward Kavanagh, and John Otis. Governor John Davis of Massachusetts sent a three-member delegation. Ashburton, realizing that he needed his own team of experts, asked Colebrooke to send him Warden James A. MacLauchlan, Alfred Reade, Colebrooke's private secretary and son-in-law, and Charles Simonds, speaker of the legislative assembly and a prominent businessman. Sir John Caldwell, the Grand Falls lumberman, also met with Ashburton and gave him advice.

The fate of the Madawaska settlement was one of the most difficult parts of the negotiations. Maine wanted the compromise border to follow the St. John River, which meant that the settlement would be split by an international border. Ashburton pushed hard to have all of the Madawaska settlement remain within British territory. In fact, the negotiations almost stalled on this point. Several options were proposed. Ashburton suggested that the boundary in that area follow a line drawn from the intersection of the Commissioners' Line and the Aroostook River to the Fish River. If

Following the ratification of the Ashburton-Webster Treaty in 1842, the new border was surveyed and boundary markers, such as this one, were placed along it. Collection of the Fredericton Region Museum and the York-Sunbury Historical Society

agreed, this would keep the Madawaska settlement intact. In return for this, Maine wanted territorial concessions, such as the narrow strip of land east of the Commissioners' Line running south from its junction with the St. John to the Eel River at Meductic. When word of this proposal reached New Brunswick, the inhabitants of the area promptly petitioned the lieutenant-governor, expressing their wish to remain within the province as British citizens. Alternatively, Maine might have accepted Grand Manan and Campobello islands in exchange. In the end, none of these options was viable: Maine prevailed by insisting that the St. John form the border through the Madawaska settlement. And with this decision both parties agreed to the new boundary.

The line thus followed the partition defined by the "garrison period," with the notable exception of the southern portion of the Madawaska settlement: the Acadians living there could become Americans or move. The United States received 7,015 square miles of the former Disputed Territory, Britain 5,012—893 more than in the 1831 arbitration. Maine got free access to the St. John River system to float its timber to market. The US government paid each state $150,000 in compensation for their surrendered land claims. Maine was also reimbursed for the cost of the Aroostook War. Lastly, the Disputed Territory Fund was divided equally between Maine and Massachusetts.

Not surprisingly, John Baker surfaced during the negotiations. He had been an ardent supporter of Maine for more than two decades, but his land would now be on the British side of the boundary. One proposal was to place an interruption in the boundary that would encompass his land; the compromise solution was a side-bar agreement that the British would purchase his land at a fair price should Baker wish to sell and move to Maine.

Following this agreement, the rest of the negotiations — dealing with the border between Lake Superior and Lake of the Woods, cooperation between the US Navy and the Royal Navy to suppress the slave trade, and the extradition of suspected criminals — went surprisingly well. The more difficult question of the Oregon Territory was not addressed. The treaty was signed on August 9, 1842, and ratified by the United States on August 22 and by Britain on October 13. The treaty had its opponents on both sides of the Atlantic. In Britain, the debate became particularly heated, and it was discussed in the press for several months before Parliament next sat. Another "battle of the maps" broke out. Besides the maps supporting the British claim, another map, attributed to Oswald, one of the British commissioners in Paris, turned up with a line drawn on it that supposedly justified the fullest extent of the American claim. In April and May 1843, the fractious discussions were finally ended when both Houses of Parliament passed motions expressing their approval of Lord Ashburton's work.

The provisions of the Ashburton-Webster Treaty were gradually implemented over the next few years. An American survey conducted by Major Graham in 1840 had detected a deviation in the line north of Monument. When this was resurveyed after the treaty, it was discovered that the cut line had followed a trial line that had been laid out by surveyors in 1817, and not a true north line. The true line ran slightly more to the east, giving Maine an additional sliver of land. One of the commissioners settling resulting land claims in the Woodstock area was MacLaughlan; later, he and

Judge Sir John Allen Campbell surveyed land claims in the Madawaska settlement. In 1842, Baker considered selling his property and asked the New Brunswick government for an evaluation, but later changed his mind. In an ironic turn of fate, John Baker, an ardent supporter of Maine, resigned himself to being a British subject.

The real tragedy was the division of the Madawaska settlement. The settlement extended from above Grand Falls along both sides of the St. John River for some distance above the Madawaska. In 1840, it had about 3,500 inhabitants. The British considered the American settlers around Baker Brook and the Fish River to be part of the Madawaska settlement, while the Americans, particularly Maine, assumed the settlement did not extend much above the Madawaska River — at least not on the southern bank of the St. John. King William's arbitration of 1831 had proposed a boundary that ran along the centre of the St. John, thus dividing the community in two. At first, because the United States rejected the arbitration, the proposed division had not become an issue. Now it was. In practical terms, the imposed boundary had little initial effect on the inhabitants of the Madawaska settlement. They remained part of the same socio-economic community, tied together by common bonds of kinship, religion, and language. In some ways it was an improvement. Except for those living on Crown Lands grants, the rest of the inhabitants were legally squatters; now, Maine and New Brunswick could give them proper deeds to the lands they lived on. As time passed, however, the divide widened, and each side of the river became more reflective of the US and British administrative systems that governed them. Still, until the events of September 11, 2001, the border was more a formality than a barrier, and a sense of shared community and shared history remains.

The garrisons lingered for a time after the treaty was signed. Those in Fort Fairfield and Fort Kent remained until 1843 and 1844, respectively, when the troops were withdrawn to Hancock Barracks in Houlton. In 1845, the post at Houlton was closed, ostensibly as part of preparations for the Mexican War of 1846-1848. In September 1843, the British garrisons in Madawaska and Fort Ingall departed, while those in Woodstock and Grand Falls remained until December 1847.

The lasting legacy, however, is the Grand Communications Route.

The British strategy to secure it was validated twenty years later during the American Civil War. On November 8, 1861, the US Navy boarded the British mail steamer *Trent* in the Bermuda passage and forcibly removed two Confederate commissioners who were *en route* to Britain and France, precipitating the "Trent Affair." The diplomatic crisis that ensued brought the two nations to the brink of war yet again. While the crisis was being defused, Britain began a massive reinforcement of British North America, sending a total of 11,500 troops between December 1861 and March 1862. Because of the season, the St. Lawrence was closed to navigation, so more than six thousand eight hundred troops travelled the Grand Communications Route through New Brunswick to Quebec.

Conclusion

The Aroostook War and the Maine-New Brunswick border dispute from 1783 to 1843 remain virtually unknown in studies of the history of North America and Anglo-American relations. Most of the history of the dispute has been written from a Maine perspective, because it seems to have had the most significance for Maine. In Maine history books written in the run-up to the centennial of statehood in 1920, the general theme was that Maine struggled valiantly and alone against the British to secure its legacy of the Disputed Territory and received little support from the government in Washington. The interpretation is partially correct, but it is not the whole story.

Curiously, the study of the Maine-New Brunswick border dispute has never been fully developed from a New Brunswick or British perspective. At the time of the Treaty of Paris, the borderland between the Massachusetts District of Maine and the British colony of Nova Scotia to the north was a vast and uncharted wilderness. Its routes and portages were well known to the aboriginal people and to the few intrepid colonists who used the St. John and Madawaska rivers to travel between the sea and the St. Lawrence. But the area was sparsely settled by Europeans, and the British negotiators were only dimly aware of its strategic importance as the sole winter route to the interior.

Benjamin Franklin and Baron von Steuben, however, seem to have understood, and their proposal that the whole watershed of the St. John be part of one jurisdiction made perfect sense. Franklin's understanding of the strategic importance of the area may have led the American negotiators to push for a boundary that denied this route to a future enemy. Unlike their negotiators, the British military were certainly aware of the strategic importance of the route and took actions to secure it, the wording of the Treaty of Paris notwithstanding. Carleton's vision of a line of military settlements along its course was vindicated when the descendants of the Loyalist regiments and the veterans of the War of 1812 stood together to defend the route during the Aroostook War.

The Aroostook War was Maine's response to the growing realization by the US and British governments that a compromise boundary was the only viable solution to the border dispute. It was also the state's response to its immediate financial crisis. Efforts had been ongoing for almost fifty-six years to find the boundary that was poorly described in the 1783 Treaty of Paris. Nearly settled by force in 1814, the Treaty of Ghent restored the land conquered by the British to the United States and returned the border issue to its unsettled state. The geography of the land simply did not match the words in the treaty. Once Maine achieved statehood, it was relentless in pressing its claim. The United States, in response to pressure from Maine, managed to persuade Britain to agree to a ban on cutting timber within the Disputed Territory. An Anglo-American understanding that development within the territory should be frozen where it was when the Treaty of Ghent was signed in 1814 was also in place. Of course, this was simply not possible as the Madawaska settlement increased in size, American citizens settled above it along the St. John River, and a mixed group of British and American citizens arrived along the Aroostook River. The British, represented by New Brunswick, also believed they had an agreement with the United States acknowledging that they were to exercise jurisdiction within the Disputed Territory. Maine rejected this understanding, and on several occasions tried, without success, to extend its jurisdiction to the region. For most of the era, the Disputed Territory was too remote for Maine to influence it directly, while the area — as Franklin had observed — formed a natural extension of what is now New Brunswick, especially the St. John River basin. To correct this, Maine began a program of road building and settlement to extend its influence to the Aroostook River, and later to the Fish River. Massachusetts, which owned half of the public lands in the area, joined in this initiative.

While this was occurring, Maine must have taken a close look at the situation and realized that its claim to all of the Disputed Territory did not have a reasonable expectation of success. Because of the need to secure and protect the Grand Communications Route, the British had decided to occupy the northern half of the Disputed Territory permanently, no matter the outcome of the boundary negotiations. Following the Americans' rejection of King William's arbitration in 1831, which Maine had orchestrated, the United States and Britain began to consider a conventional or compromise boundary agreement. The political leaders of Maine realized that, if Maine was to be successful in any of its claim to the Disputed Territory, it had to act. Buckmore's report that there would be extensive cutting of trespass timber during the winter of 1838/1839 gave them their justification. Although the Aroostook War threatened to spin out of control and to start an Anglo-American War, the results gave Maine what it wanted—control of part of the Disputed Territory. Using the traditional tactic of "bite and hold," Maine consolidated its control of the Aroostook Valley and used it as a springboard to occupy the Fish River area.

With the Maine land agent's Corps of Volunteers having effective control of the area south of the St. John, except for the part of the Madawaska settlement along the right bank of the river, the Disputed Territory was partitioned. Both sides dug in and were not likely to be dislodged no matter what the diplomats in Washington and London thought. This period, from 1839 to 1842, was characterized by the military and paramilitary occupation of the Disputed Territory. So, when Ashburton and Webster met in Washington in the summer of 1842, there was not much room for negotiation. The partitioning of the Disputed Territory essentially decided the terms of their Ashburton-Webster Treaty, at least that part of it pertaining to the Maine-New Brunswick border.

In the end, Maine played a critical role because it had the most to lose by inaction. Finding a timely resolution to the boundary dispute was not a high priority for Washington or for London. The British had achieved their strategic goal by occupying the northern half of the Disputed Territory and securing the Grand Communications Route, the importance of which diminished only with the building of railways. Even then, the final settlement of the border left little room for an all-British railway line to the Canadas: in the 1870s, when the Inter-Colonial railway was built, it crossed New Brunswick and Quebec as far east, and as far away from the United States, as possible.

For its part, New Brunswick had no reason to push for a quick settlement. The crucial portion of the Disputed Territory was soon settled, and British subjects were drifting up the region's rivers through natural growth. Moreover, the only route to market for the area's timber was down the St. John. Even the final awarding of the southern portion of the Disputed Territory did not change the economic realities of the timber trade. Maine had to counter this by expanding its roads and settlement into the area and, by doing so, enforce its claim by physical occupation of the ground. All of this came to a head in the months of February and March 1839, when the border crisis, known as the Aroostook War, changed the dynamics of the border dispute forever.

The international boundary between Maine and New Brunswick is the legacy of the Aroostook War and the ensuing partitioning of the Disputed Territory that culminated in the Ashburton-Webster Treaty. The garrison period is remembered today by the continuing presence of some of the fortifications that were built at Fort Fairfield, Fort Kent, Edmundston, and Cabano. Regrettably, the posts at Grand Falls and Dégelis have disappeared over time. The question of who won the Aroostook War still occasionally arises. Maine gained control of the Aroostook Valley, and so won that round. In the broader view, however, both sides had compromised during the treaty negotiations and so both had won. The white pine timber that was Maine's prize has largely disappeared, replaced by potatoes and pulpwood. Only the divided Madawaska settlement — now even more firmly separated by post 9/11 security measures along America's borders — remains as an unfortunate legacy of an otherwise reasonable and largely peaceful settlement of the dispute. And the Grand Communications Route continues to serve in its new configuration as the Trans-Canada Highway.

.75 calibre smoothbore India Pattern musket, standard weapon of the British army from the 1790s until the 1850s, with some militia units continuing to use it until the 1860s. Collection of the Fredericton Region Museum and the York-Sunbury Historical Society

.69 calibre smoothbore Model 1816 musket, used by US regular army and state militia troops during the Aroostook War. Courtesy of the National Firearms Museum

.65 calibre Baker rifle, introduced in 1800 and used by the rifle companies attached to some New Brunswick militia battalions during the Aroostook War. NBM 1601

Appendix

Weaponry of the Aroostook War

During the Aroostook War, the British had the transportation advantage, while Maine had the edge on armament. The main weapon on both sides was a smooth-bore, flintlock musket. The British used the India Pattern musket, their mainstay during the War of 1812, until it was replaced starting in the 1840s — it was issued to some militia units until the 1860s. It had a 39-inch barrel, was .75 calibre, and fired a slightly smaller ball to facilitate loading. The Americans used muskets that originally had been modelled on French firearms of the Revolutionary War period. The Maine militia most likely used a variation of the Model 1816 US Flintlock musket. It had a 42-inch barrel, was .69 calibre, and again fired a slightly smaller ball. Many New Brunswick militia battalions had a rifle company attached to them. It is not known for certain how they were armed, but they likely carried Baker rifles. Introduced in 1800, these had a 30-inch barrel and were .65 calibre. The troops of cavalry likely were armed with swords and pistols. Based on examples in provincial collections, the swords were probably the outdated Pattern 1796 Light Cavalry ones. The officers would have carried the standard Pattern Infantry Officers' sword or another pattern authorized for their particular corps, such as the artillery. US cavalry and militia officers would have carried swords similar to those of their counterparts in the US Army.

The American arms industry, however, gave the Maine riflemen a distinct edge. Starting in 1817, the army had adopted the Model 1819 Hall breech-loading rifle. It was a .52 calibre rifle with a 32 5/8-inch barrel. The breech tipped up for loading and then pushed down to align it with the barrel for firing. With a higher rate of fire than a muzzle-loader and the ability to easily reload while lying in the prone position or otherwise protected from hostile fire, this gave the riflemen a decided advantage. Many Maine rifle companies, such as the Hancock Guards under Captain Charles H. Wing, were equipped with this rifle. Indeed, the arms race had the potential to escalate. On February 27, E.B. Zabriskie wrote to Maine's Governor Fairfield on behalf of the Patent Arms Manufacturing Company offering to sell him percussion Colt revolving rifles at $57.50 each. Apparently, they could provide one hundred rifles on short notice and possibly more. He also offered a six-shot carbine for cavalry but did not specify the quantity available for delivery.

Both sides also used smooth-bore, muzzle-loading brass cannon of various calibres. Troops preferred using brass guns in the field as they were lighter than their iron counterparts. While the US Army did not aid Maine directly, it appears that it did help to arm the state. On February 21, the *Bangor Whig* reported that "1700 of Hall's best Rifles are on the way from Augusta," where there was a federal arsenal. Then, on March 11, it was reported that, on March 6, "a train of wagons, carrying twenty-four field pieces, left the Watervliet Arsenal… for Maine… in obedience to orders from Washington."

Variant of the Pattern 1796 Light Cavalry sword of the type believed to have been used by cavalry troops of the New Brunswick militia.
Collection of the Fredericton Region Museum and the York-Sunbury Historical Society

.52 calibre Model 1819 Hall breech-loading rifle, used by rifle companies of the Maine militia during the Aroostook War; breech-loading meant the rifleman could fire and reload from cover, making himself less vulnerable to enemy fire and giving him a distinct advantage over British troops armed with muzzle-loaders. Courtesy of the National Firearms Museum

Acknowledgements

It all started when I married a girl from Perth-Andover, New Brunswick. I first heard about the Aroostook War when I visited her home town, and this whetted my curiosity to learn more about it. In turn, this led to my PhD dissertation about the Maine-New Brunswick border dispute, from which most of the material presented in this book is drawn. I would like to thank my supervising committee, Doctors Bill Parenteau, Marc Milner, and Stephen Turner, for their excellent work in guiding and shaping my research.

Those who helped me in my research are acknowledged in my dissertation, so I only touch on them here. I received great support from the Harriet Irving Library at the University of New Brunswick, the Provincial Archives of New Brunswick, the Legislative Library of New Brunswick, the New Brunswick Museum, Library and Archives Canada, the Acadian Archives at the University of Maine Fort Kent, the Maine State Archives, the Maine Historical Society, and the National Archives, formerly the Public Record Office, in the United Kingdom. Dr. Béatrice Craig continued to share her extensive knowledge of the Madawaska settlement with me. Lieutenant-Colonel (Retired) Bob Dallison and I shared our research on parallel projects; his suggestions for sources and reports of information were always appreciated. Greg Campbell of the L.P. Fisher Memorial Library was an excellent source of information about the Woodstock area. As the book moved into production, Marc Milner and Brent Wilson of the New Brunswick Military Heritage Project did an excellent job of editing and helping to mould my narrative into shape. Mike Bechthold produced the maps. The staff of Goose Lane Editions—in particular Angela Williams, Chris Tompkins, and Julie Scriver—and freelance editor Barry Norris helped to see the book through to final publication. Finally, I would like to thank my wife, Carolyn, for encouraging me to write this book and for gracefully accepting the inconveniences it created. Without her support, this would not have been possible.

Selected Bibliography

Bourne, Kenneth. *Britain and the Balance of Power in North America, 1815-1908.* Berkeley and Los Angeles: University of California Press, 1967.

Burrage, Henry S. *Maine in the Northeastern Boundary Controversy.* Portland, ME: Marks Printing Houses, 1919.

Campbell, W.E. (Gary). "Forts, Writs and Logs: A Reassessment of the Military, Political and Economic Dimensions of the Maine/New Brunswick Border Dispute, 1783-1843." PhD dissertation, University of New Brunswick, 2010.

———. *The Road to Canada: The Grand Communications Route from Saint John to Quebec.* Fredericton, NB: Goose Lane Editions and the New Brunswick Military Heritage Project, 2005.

Carroll, Francis M. *A Good and Wise Measure: The Search for the Canadian-American Boundary, 1783-1842.* Toronto: University of Toronto Press, 2001.

Classen, H. George. *Thrust and Counterthrust: The Genesis of the Canada-United States Boundary.* Don Mills, ON: Longmans Canada Limited, 1965.

Craig, Béatrice, Maxime Dagenais, Lisa Ornstein, and Guy Dubay. *The Land in Between: The Upper St. John Valley, Prehistory to World War I.* Gardiner, ME: Tilbury House, 2009.

Dallison, Robert L. *A Neighbourly War: New Brunswick and the War of 1812.* Fredericton, NB: Goose Lane Editions and the New Brunswick Military Heritage Project, 2012.

———. *Hope Restored: The American Revolution and the Founding of New Brunswick.* Fredericton, NB: Goose Lane Editions and the New Brunswick Military Heritage Project, 2003.

Jones, Howard. *To the Webster-Ashburton Treaty: A Study in Anglo-American Relations 1783-1843.* Chapel Hill: University of North Carolina Press, 1977.

Jones, Howard, and Donald A. Rakestraw. *Prologue to Manifest Destiny: Anglo-American Relations in the 1840s*. Wilmington, DE: Scholarly Resources, 1997.

Judd, Richard W., Edwin A. Churchill, and Joel W. Eastman, eds. *Maine: The Pine Tree State from Prehistory to the Present*. Orono: University of Maine Press, 1995.

Mann, Michael. *A Particular Duty: The Canadian Rebellions, 1837-1838*. Salisbury, UK: Michael Russell, 1986.

McNutt, W.S. *New Brunswick, A History: 1784-1867*. [1963] Toronto: Macmillan of Canada, 1984.

Poitras, Jacques. *Imaginary Line: Life on an Unfinished Border*. Fredericton, NB: Goose Lane Editions, 2011.

Scott, Geraldine Tidd. *Ties of Common Blood: A History of Maine's Northeast Boundary Dispute with Great Britain, 1783-1842*. Bowie, MD: Heritage Books, 1992.

Photo Credits

The photo on the front cover, *Fort Fairfield, July 1839* by Lieutenant Philip John Bainbrigge, Royal Engineers, appears courtesy of Library and Archives Canada. The photos of the firearms on the cover is appear courtesy of the National Firearms Museum and the Fredericton Region Museum. The maps on pages 12, 28, 46, 89, 96, and 118 appear courtesy of Mike Bechthold. The painting on page 19 (LAC C-012724), the sketch on page 41 (C115855), the painting on page 94 (LAC C-031249), the painting on page 113 (LAC C-40144), and the painting on page 117 (LAC C-017787) appear courtesy of Library and Archives Canada. The sketch on page 20 appears courtesy of the Maine State Archives. The three photos on page 25 (from top to bottom, 380186 (3), 30145 (2) and 301442), the sketch on page 58 (W701(1)), and the bottom photo on page 134 (1601) appear courtesy of the New Brunswick Museum. The painting on page 32 appears courtesy of the King's Landing Historical Settlement. The painting on page 35 appears courtesy of the artist, Esther On Faulkner and the Aroostook Historical and Art Museum, Houlton, ME. The notice on page 38 (RS63713f5) appears courtesy of the Provincial Archives of New Brunswick. The painting on page 52 is by Thomas Doney, Anthony, Edwards & Co., public domain. The painting on page 53 is by Geo. H. Walker & Co., Boston, public domain. The proclamation on page 65 appears courtesy of the Maine Historical Society. The etching on page 66 is from Col. Montgomery Maxwell, *My Adventures,* Vol. 1 (London: Henry Colburn, 1845). The drawing on page 69 is from *History of Penobscot County, Maine* (Cleveland: Williams, Chase & Co., 1882). The photo on pages 74 and 75 appears courtesy of McLauchlan's descendants. The painting on page 82 by Robert Walter Weir, appears courtesy of the Metropolitan Museum of Art. The photographs on pages 84 and 103 are by the author. The painting on page 102 appears courtesy of the Fort Fairfield Sesquicentennial Committee. The photo on page 105 appears courtesy of Andrew John Monkhouse. The map on page 108 appears courtesy of Béatrice Craig. The photo on page 109 is by Howard W. Marshall from the Maine Acadian Cultural Survey Collection and appears courtesy of the American Folklife Center, Library of Congress, Washington DC. The drawing on page 114, original sketch by Lieutenant Philip John Bainbrigge, Royal Engineers, adapted by Béatrice Craig appears courtesy of Béatrice Craig. The paintings on pages 121 and 123 appear courtesy of the Library of Congress. The photo on page 125, the top photo on page 134, and the top photo on page 137 appear courtesy of the Collection of the Fredericton Region Museum and the York-Sunbury Historical Society. The middle photo on page 134 and the bottom photo on page 137 appear courtesy of the National Firearms Museum. All illustrative material is reproduced by permission.

Index

Bloodless Aroostook War 11
Bonaparte, Napoleon 20, 21
Boston MA 84
Bouchette, Colonel Joseph 23
Boundary Commission 18, 25, 36
Bridgewater ME 86, 90
Bristol NB 18, 23, 26, 73, 90
British Army
    Commissariat Department 79, 111
British Army, Militia
    3rd Provisional Battalion 81
    Carleton County Militia 75
        1st Battalion 60, 64, 73, 90, 95
        2nd Battalion 64, 73, 74, 88, 89,
            101
        3rd Battalion 88
    Carleton Light Dragoons 77, 88
    Charlotte County Militia
        1st Battalion 91
        2nd Battalion 76
        4th Battalion 91
    City Guard of Saint John 75
    City Rifle Battalion 76
    Cornwall Light Infantry 81
    New Brunswick Militia Artillery 90,
        91, 95
    New Brunswick Regiment of
        Artillery 76
    Quebec Volunteer Cavalry 81
    Saint John City Militia 90
        1st Battalion 76
    Woodstock Rifle Company 77, 95
    York County Militia 75, 90
        1st Battalion 76
        2nd Battalion 76
        3rd Battalion 76
    York Hussars 95
    York Light Dragoons 90, 98
British Army, Provincial Corps
    Arnold's American Legion 16
    Delancey's Brigade

    1st Battalion 16
    2nd Battalion 16
    Guides 16
    King's American Dragoons 16
    King's American Regiment 16
    Loyal American Regiment 16
    Maryland Loyalists 16
    New Jersey Volunteers
        1st Battalion 16
        2nd Battalion 16
    New York Volunteers 16
    Pennsylvania Loyalists 16
    Pioneers 16
    Prince of Wales's American
        Regiment 16
    Queen's Rangers 16
British Army, Regulars and Fencibles
    8th (King's) Regiment of Foot
        2nd Battalion 21
    10th Royal Veterans Regiment 23
    11th (North Devonshire) Regiment
        of Foot 78
    11th Regiment 43, 87, 88, 90, 98, 112
    15th Regiment of Foot 112
    34th Regiment 42
    36th (Herefordshire) Regiment of
        Foot 67, 70, 72, 73, 74, 78, 88, 89,
        90, 95, 98
    43rd Regiment of Foot 40, 41, 42
    52nd Regiment of Foot 104
    56th Regiment 115, 116
    65th Regiment 43, 90
    69th (South Lincolnshire) Regiment
        of Foot 78, 88, 90, 95, 98, 101,
        107, 110
    85th Regiment 42
    93rd Regiment 90
    95th Regiment 43
    98th (Prince of Wales's Tipperary
        Regiment) Regiment of Foot 23

104th (New Brunswick) Regiment of
Foot 21, 23, 74, 107
King's New Brunswick Regiment 18
New Brunswick Fencibles 23
Royal Artillery 67, 78, 88, 89, 90, 91,
95, 98
4th Battalion (1st Company) 43
4th Battalion (8th Company) 42
Royal Engineers 47, 58, 101, 103,
108, 111, 112, 114, 117
Royal West Indian Rangers 23
British Emancipation Act of 1833 120
British North America 13, 14, 23, 77,
83, 113, 120, 128
Buckmore, George W. 50, 51, 54, 61,
72, 106, 131
Bull, Peter 55
Burton, William J. 109
Buttermilk Creek NB 73, 74, 90

C

Cabano QC 15, 42, 112, 132
Calais ME 77, 91, 95
Caldwell, Sir John 111, 124
Campbell, Lieutenant-Governor
Major-General Sir Archibald 38,
78
Campbell, Lieutenant-Governor Sir
Colin 77, 78
Campbell, Judge Sir John Allen 127
Campobello Island NB 125
Canada Command 77
Canada Line of the Great Road 42
Canterbury NB 54
Caribou ME 51, 56, 84
Carleton, Lieutenant-Governor
Thomas 17, 18, 130
Caroline 119, 120
Cary, Shepard 79, 100, 106
Castine ME 22
census 29, 38, 40, 42, 112

Chambly QC 78, 88
Chambre, Brevet Major William 112
Champlain, Samuel de 14, 23
Cherokee First Nation 81
Chipman, Ward 14, 24, 29
Clay, Henry 29
Clements, Captain George 76
Coffin, George W. 30, 31, 33, 50, 61, 66
Colborne, Governor-General Sir John
77, 78, 111, 112, 115
Colebrooke, Sir William 116, 124
Commissioners' Line 9, 19, 23, 25, 29,
34, 44, 55, 56, 66, 73, 80, 86, 87,
98, 105, 110, 124, 125
Connecticut River 14
Coombs, Leonard 38, 39
Coote, Captain 107
Creole 120
Crown Lands Office 31, 43
Cummings, Lieutenant-Colonel
George W. 86
Cunliffe, Captain Elisha A. 60
Cunliffe, Captain Thomas G. 73
Cushman, Gustavus G. 9, 53, 55, 56, 58

D

Daveis, Charles Steward 34, 35
Davis, Governor John 124
Deane, John E. 38, 46, 47
Dégelis QC 23, 42, 111, 114, 115, 132
Demill, Captain Rufus S. 77
Diblee, John 60
Disputed Territory 9, 10, 12, 17, 24, 26,
27, 29, 30-39, 41-49, 51, 54, 57, 58,
60, 61, 66, 67, 69, 71, 72, 79, 83,
85, 88, 91, 93, 97, 103, 106, 107,
110-113, 115, 117, 118, 122, 124,
125, 129-132
Disputed Territory Fund 32, 68, 126
Douglas, Lieutenant-Governor Sir
Howard 35

The New Brunswick Military History Museum

The mission of the New Brunswick Military History Museum is to collect, preserve, research, and exhibit artifacts which illustrate the history and heritage of the military forces in New Brunswick and New Brunswickers at war, during peacetime, and on United Nations or North Atlantic Treaty Organization duty.

The New Brunswick Military History Museum is proud to partner with the Gregg Centre.

Highlighting 400 years of New Brunswick's history.

www.nbmilitaryhistorymuseum.ca
info@nbmilitaryhistorymuseum.ca

The New Brunswick Military Heritage Project

The New Brunswick Military Heritage Project, a non-profit organization devoted to public awareness of the remarkable military heritage of the province, is an initiative of the Brigadier Milton F. Gregg, VC, Centre for the Study of War and Society of the University of New Brunswick. The organization consists of museum professionals, teachers, university professors, graduate students, active and retired members of the Canadian Forces, and other historians. We welcome public involvement. People who have ideas for books or information for our database can contact us through our website: www.unb.ca/nbmhp.

One of the main activities of the New Brunswick Military Heritage Project is the publication of the New Brunswick Military Heritage Series with Goose Lane Editions. This series of books is under the direction of J. Brent Wilson, Director of the New Brunswick Military Heritage Project at the University of New Brunswick. Publication of the series is supported by a grant from the Canadian War Museum.

The New Brunswick Military Heritage Series

Volume 1
Saint John Fortifications, 1630-1956,
Roger Sarty and Doug Knight

Volume 2
*Hope Restored: The American Revolution and the Founding
of New Brunswick,* Robert L. Dallison

Volume 3
The Siege of Fort Beauséjour, 1755, Chris M. Hand

Volume 4
*Riding into War: The Memoir of a Horse Transport Driver,
1916-1919,* James Robert Johnston

Volume 5
*The Road to Canada: The Grand Communications Route
from Saint John to Quebec,* W.E. (Gary) Campbell

Volume 6
*Trimming Yankee Sails: Pirates and Privateers of
New Brunswick,* Faye Kert

Volume 7
*War on the Home Front: The Farm Diaries of
Daniel MacMillan, 1914-1927,*
edited by Bill Parenteau and Stephen Dutcher

About the Author

Major (Retired) W.E. (Gary) Campbell served as an army officer for over forty-two years in the Canadian Army (Militia), Canadian Army (Regular), and the Canadian Forces. As a transportation officer in the Logistics Branch, he was employed in a variety of line and staff positions in navy, army, air force, and headquarters units across Canada and in the United States and the United Kingdom. He has a Bachelor of Arts (History) from the University of Western Ontario, a Master of Arts (War Studies) from the Royal Military College of Canada, and a Doctor of Philosophy (History) from the University of New Brunswick. His dissertation was titled "Forts, Writs and Logs: A Reassessment of the Military, Political and Economic Dimensions of the Maine/New Brunswick Border Dispute, 1783-1843," which includes a detailed examination of the historical background and events of the Aroostook War. He is also the author of *The Road to Canada: The Grand Communications Route from Saint John to Quebec*, volume 5 in the New Brunswick Military Heritage Project book series.

Gary Campbell has a passion for military history, with a logistics flavour, and has written articles for several journals on this subject. An active member of the Orders and Medals Research Society, the Military Collectors Club of Canada, and the York-Sunbury Historical Society, he has served as a member of the board of the latter two groups. A member of the Royal Canadian Legion, he serves as a volunteer with the Dominion Command in Ottawa as the Medals Advisor. He is currently expanding his interest in genealogy as he researches his Planter and Loyalist ancestors.

He and his wife Carolyn Jamer, a former military nurse, have been married for over thirty-nine years. They presently reside in the Fredericton, New Brunswick area. Carolyn is from Perth-Andover, the heartland of the

Aroostook War, and inspired his interest in this subject. They have two married daughters, one is a chartered accountant and the other is an RCAF officer with a Master's degree in aerospace engineering. Two sons-in-law and three wonderful grandchildren round out their family. In retirement, they have pursued their interest in travel with an emphasis on cruising.